MICRO-MYTHS

Exploring the Limits of Learning with Computers

Joe Nathan

WINSTON PRESS

By the same author
Free to Teach (Winston Press)

The author is grateful for permission to reprint material originally published in somewhat different form:

"A Computer Specialist at Work." Reprinted with permission from the March 1984 issue of *Learning Magazine*. Copyright © by the Springhouse Corporation.

"Minnesota Act Mandates Schools Utilize Technology." Reprinted with permission from the December 5, 1983, issue of *Infoworld*, 1060 Marsh Rd., Menlo Park, Calif. 94025. Copyright © 1983 by Popular Computing, Inc., a subsidiary of CW Communications, Inc.

"Teaching Tips," "Research about Computers," and "The Myth of the All-Powerful Machine." Reprinted with permission from, respectively, the December 1984, the March 1985, and the June 1985 issues of *Computer User*. Copyright © by MSP Publications, Inc.

"Tommorrow's Visifarmers." Reprinted with permission from the June 1984 issue of *Family Computing*. Copyright © by Scholastic, Inc.

Cover design: Terry Dugan

Library of Congress Catalog Card Number: 85-51014

ISBN: 0-86683-967-4

Printed in the United States of America

5 4 3 2 1

Winston Press, Inc.
430 Oak Grove
Minneapolis, Minnesota 55403

CONTENTS

ACKNOWLEDGMENTS

Many people think a painter and author work in much the same way. They believe that both work alone, with little outside contact, until they are finally satisfied. And then they let the world see their product.

It doesn't work that way for this author. Many people have been generous and gracious to me as I prepared this book. First, my thanks to Russell Ewald, Arthur Himmelman, and the board of the McKnight Foundation, which provided funds that supported my research, thinking, and writing. Without their assistance, this book could not have been written.

More than 200 people from around the country talked with me about various aspects of computing. Most of them are acknowledged in the Resources section, but I want to particularly thank the educators and young people in Blue Earth, Bermuda, Chicago, Fairbanks, Hartford, Houston, Minneapolis, Ortonville, Oxford, and St. Paul.

As a book is written, knowledgeable people can help an author by challenging her or him to clarify, strengthen, or revise portions of the book. Wayne Paulson at Winston Press welcomed my ideas. Editor Tom Grady patiently, persistently helped clarify and tighten the book. The following people provided detailed comments and suggestions: Tom Gregory, Beverly Hunter, Wayne Jennings, Mitch Pearlstein, Don Rawitsch, Linda Roberts, Marc Tucker, and Gil Valdez. The book is infinitely better because of their assistance.

I'm particularly indebted to Linda Mohn, a marvelous kindergarten teacher at St. Paul's Horace Mann Elementary School, who welcomed my discussions with and observations of her students.

My father, C. Henry Nathan, has encouraged me for thirty five years to do my best.

Our children, David and Elizabeth, patiently taught their father a great deal about the world view of six-year-olds. I hope this book will help them create a better world.

JoAnn Lukesh Nathan is a constant joy in my life. Her insight, humor, patience, and vision make my life much better. I am deeply grateful to her.

So I have not worked alone. Each of these people helped. I hope this book justifies their assistance.

1

INTRODUCTION

As a parent, an educator, and a taxpayer, I hope that personal computers will help make dramatic improvements in the ways youngsters learn. However, if present trends continue, it seems unlikely that these machines will fulfill their potential.

It's easy, of course, to find claims that technology will transform education. Consider the following statement by the highest-ranking federal educator:

> [Our office] is called upon to answer a constant stream of inquiries on the vital subject of _____, which touches so many phases of life. From the remote regions and from the cosmopolitan areas, from amateurs, from professors, from students, from advertisers, from reformers and those who need reforming, questions pour in. . . . The _____ has captivated the imagination of the entire civilized world. It is stimulating a new revival of learning (Cooper, p. 29).

In this case, U.S. Commissioner of Education William John Cooper was speaking in 1932 of the *radio*, not the computer.

Some years later, another authority wrote:

> The _____ permits the learner to learn faster and in a different way. _____ is a new technique that may revolutionize teaching methods. Its basic principle is that students learn in small, sequential steps. On the whole _____ has tremendous potentialities to improve American education. . . . Over 100 firms are making the machines and the programs that go with them. The field is big and growing bigger. _____

can be used in schools, in homes, in adult correspondence courses, in industrial training classes, in the armed forces, and in underdeveloped countries where illiteracy is a major problem. The movement has attracted millions of dollars from the Ford Foundation, the Carnegie Corporation, and the United States Office of Education. None of these organizations is noted for throwing money away on wild schemes (Fine, pp. 5-10, 23).

That statement was made in 1962 by Dr. Benjamin Fine, former education editor of the *New York Times* and expressed enthusiasm for teaching machines and programmed learning.

Much of today's hoopla about computers and learning also surrounded earlier innovations. Claims have been made (and millions of dollars spent on) radio, television, overhead projectors, videotape recorders, motion pictures, talking typewriters, and language labs. Conferences have been held, training programs created, magazines started, articles and books written, federal and foundation money spent. Yet these machines have had little impact on the actual learning and teaching that goes on in our schools.

Machines may have made our lives easier, but probably haven't made our lives much happier. There has been widespread acceptance of technological advance, with relatively little thought about its impact on us. We need to think carefully about computers and learning.

Although I have serious reservations about computers, it would be hypocritical of me to insist that computers are worthless. After all, this book was written on a computer. But the picture is not all positive. There is enormous hype in the marketing of computers. In some schools, computers are being used in disturbing, damaging, and possibly even destructive ways. Millions of dollars are being spent by parents and educators to purchase computers and related material, with little idea of what to do with them. In this book I intend to explore not only the possibilities but also the problems computers can create.

My encounter with computers began fifteen years ago, with a college course in programming. Since then, I've worked fourteen years as a public school aide, a teacher, and an administrator. I've helped schools develop programs to use computers, and I've authored a number of articles about their use in home and school. I've worked both in urban and small-town schools, and I have visited more than a hundred schools around the United States in preparing this book. In every school, I found conflicts and concerns about computers.

As one who writes about computers, I receive many questions on the subject. Knowing that my wife, JoAnn, and I are parents of six-year-old twins, people often ask whether we think they should buy a computer for their children. There is a mixture of fear and curiosity in most of the questions—a desire to find out what's best for one's children, without knowing exactly what questions to ask. It is critical for us to discuss appropriate roles for computers. It is vital for us to review what questions we should be asking. If we don't ask the right questions, we'll certainly get the wrong answers. For example, if people ask, "What computer should I buy for my young children?" they will get various answers. But if parents ask, "Should I buy a computer for my child *now*?" the answers will be quite different. If educators ask, "What is computer literacy?" they will get various responses. But perhaps the entire concept of computer literacy should be questioned. Educators might instead ask, "What are the most important ways to use computers in schools?"

In *Micro-Myths*, I want to explore a number of myths commonly held about computers and learning:

1. Computers are neutral—they're just another tool.
2. There is such a thing as computer literacy, and every graduate of our schools needs to have it.
3. Using computers is the most effective way for most students to learn most subjects.

4. Computers will revolutionize our schools.
5. The lessons of the past about introducing new technology into schools are clear and obvious.
6. All responsible parents who can possibly afford it should buy computers for their children.
7. There is not much software that can be used effectively to increase learning.

These assertions, in fact, may not be true. Nobel Prize-winning scientist Herbert Simon recently described the importance of understanding the true significance of innovations. He recalled that although people originally thought automobiles would be important for carrying things from one place to another, the true significance of the car was in its "creation of the suburbs, and its creation of the 2,000-mile vacation, complete with children and dog" (Simon, p. 18). That is, cars made it possible for people to live notable distances from their work, and for families to travel far from their homes.

Similarly, it's important for us to understand the computer's true significance. But authorities don't agree on what that significance is.

- Some people envision computers as *substitute teachers* who make learning more enjoyable for young people and who are cheaper and more patient than the average classroom teacher.
- Some say that computers should function as *workbooks* that take over dull jobs, thus freeing humans to do more creative tasks. These people argue that computers can drill students endlessly, permit youngsters to move at their own pace, and provide the kind of individual attention that a certified teacher does not have time to offer.
- Some experts feel computers represent a new *language* that citizens must master in order to be literate.
- Some authorities ridicule the notion of computer literacy and see the computer more as a *pencil*. They consider it a tool that can be used to help accomplish various tasks.

- And some of us would like computers to be viewed as *rockets*—devices that, properly used, can help take people places few of us have been before. Improperly used, however, computers can be destructive and dangerous.

This book is not intended to resolve all these disagreements. However, I *do* question much of the "prevailing wisdom" about the effective use of computers. My purpose is to help parents, educators, and policymakers think carefully about appropriate and inappropriate uses of computers. The book describes ways in which computers can be used to bring schools and communities closer together; shows how computers can be used to stimulate, challenge, encourage, and motivate learning; points to other institutional arrangements that inhibit effective use of computer power; and presents the cases of people who have known how to use computers well, but have been prevented from doing so.

Experts often point fingers at educators for resisting change, and there certainly is some truth to that accusation. But many of the most creative and important ideas about computers and learning come from schools, where teachers and kids are doing things the experts didn't believe could happen. And so there is a strong plea in this book to turn the disdain so many experts hold for teachers into appreciation.

The most advanced, effective use of computers requires rethinking attitudes, providing opportunities for creative experimentation, and changing traditional patterns and practices. Computers can do much, but they cannot do these tasks for us-we must be open, thoughtful, and brave enough to do them ourselves.

2

COMPUTER HYPE

Getting information about computers is easy. Getting *accurate* information is not. Parents and educators are deluged with advertising claims. They are invited to conferences, often set up by companies simply to promote the use of their own equipment or educational materials. In order to make informed decisions about the use of computers, we must learn to distinguish advertising puffery from appropriate proposals. This chapter describes some of the claims currently being made about computers.

Most twentieth-century technological innovations have had little lasting impact on schools. It's almost impossible to find a talking typewriter. Most schools have taken out their language laboratories. Few schools use radios for anything except background music. A relatively small number of teachers use movie projectors as a supplement to their class lessons. In most schools, television sets sit quietly off ninety percent of the time. Unfortunately, no technological innovation during the last fifty years has changed the fundamental organization or structure of our nation's schools.

But the hope persists that technology will revolutionize our schools. The editors of *Personal Computing* suggested in September 1984, "Computers may yet save our schools." . . .

Representative Albert Gore, Jr., of Tennessee, author of the 1984 National Educational Software Act, says, "The potential for computers to improve education is enormous—more dramatic than any invention since writing" (Bonner, p. 67).

Many people, including educators, buy the hype, then buy the computers without a clear idea of what will be done with them. The National School Boards Association recently polled its members about computers. It found that virtually all school districts have purchased computers and software for instructional use, but just fourteen percent of them have any policies guiding their purchases; eighty-six percent of districts don't have a policy. It's enough to start another taxpayers' revolution (National School Boards Association, pp. 1-3).

The hype about computers isn't confined to their use in schools. Parents are constantly being urged to purchase computers for their homes so as not to cheat their children. One nationally shown advertisement for computers depicts a group of adults at a party, talking about buying a computer to help their children in school. One parent says that she wouldn't know where to start. Another parent replies, "We know how you feel, but felt we had to do something." The first adult says she would be afraid to buy, knowing so little about computers. The second speaker responds, "I was afraid to buy a home computer, but I was more afraid not to!"

Another commercial shows a parent and teacher talking about the parent's daughter. Apparently the child is not doing well in school, not working up to her potential. The teacher shows the parent several assignments that have not been done well, and the parent says she doesn't know what to do. Then, instead of asking if there are any problems at home that might have contributed to the daughter's poor performance, the teacher in this little drama asks, "Have you thought about buying a home computer?"

Advertising about computers is more exaggerated than honorable. A national software company states that parents can "send your kids to a better college for under $100" by purchasing their software. The company's ad proclaims, "Not only will it improve their test-taking skills, it will improve their scores." No qualifications, no maybes—it *will* improve their scores. Yet another software producer promises: "How to get better grades at any age. . . . We'll teach your children to spell 4,000 words by the time they're 14 years old."

The examples of overstated computer claims are endless. The advertising situation is so bad that one of the best major national computing magazines, *Infoworld*, featured a weekly award for the computer "overreacher of the week."

Though unfortunate, this kind of advertising appears to be having an impact. A national market research corporation, TALMIS, investigates consumers' buying patterns. One of their recent studies showed that the number of households with home computers doubled during the last three months of 1983. More than three million households purchased computers during the last quarter of 1983. The company expected the number of households with computers to double again during 1984 (TALMIS, p. 7). However, the number of families owning computers did *not* double in that year. Many people resented the heavy-handed advertising and were not sure what impact computers would have.

Knowing whom to trust to recommend software is a real problem for consumers. Because there are thousands of software packages available, producers have difficulty getting their products noticed, and some companies are using questionable approaches to attract attention. One firm has offered to pay free-lance reviewers fifty dollars for any detailed review of its product that appears in print (Dyrli, p. 11). *Infoworld* recently lamented that "[software] buyers . . . are in trouble. They are finding they must fend for themselves in a sea of claims, counterclaims, and confusion" (*Infoworld*, July 16, 1984, p. 37).

But even the computer magazines aren't always a source of helpful information because it's extremely difficult for computer users to know which publications to trust. One problem is that so many magazines started with a flourish and then died within eighteen months. More than a dozen national computer publications ceased operations in the last several years. There are certain publications that maintain high standards of integrity, but consumers often aren't sure which ones they are.

This summary of advertising doesn't mean to portray "hype" as the fundamental problem. It's not. The advertising is effective because people are worried, uncertain, and confused. They want their children/students to succeed. They don't want to be viewed as old-fashioned. Middle- and upper-class parents want youngsters to have every advantage, every opportunity. (Many educators report enormous pressure from these parents to buy computers.) Advocates for low-income students and for blacks, Hispanics, and Native Americans demand that these children not be left behind as victims of technological revolutions. Equity is quite properly a deep concern.

There is a grave danger that computers will not be allowed to reach their potential in schools because there is so much misinformation, so much exaggeration, so strong a push to purchase them without clear, intelligent plans for their use, and so much resistance to institutional change.

Parents and professional educators should question the pressure to place computers in every classroom. Legislators should examine the pressures to mandate computer literacy for students and for prospective and present educators. It's time to carefully review the possibilities, evaluate different approaches, and make decisions based on solid information, not on computer hype. And so this book is directed at parents *and* professional educators, in hopes of encouraging and assisting them.

And that brings us back to the seven popular myths prevalent about computers. Are they just part of the hype surrounding computers and learning? Throughout the rest of this book, I will examine these myths in detail and try to separate what is true about each statement from what is merely overstatement.

MYTH 1: Computers are neutral — they're just another tool.

3

HOW COMPUTERS AFFECT OUR VIEW OF THE WORLD

At first reading, the notion that computers are neutral and just another technological tool may seem quite a reasonable one. The tendency is to nod one's head in agreement. Computers are just powerful tools that people will use as they see fit.

But can any technological innovation that comes into widespread use be neutral? Think of the influence the automobile and television have had on our culture. The evidence is accumulating that computers are having a decided impact on the way our schools and society organize, communicate, and make decisions. The following vignettes, all of them true, help illustrate ways computers are affecting our thinking.

*　　*　　*

A group of top education officials met with a software producer for a large corporation, who showed the officials some programs that were designed to help expand students' creativity and improve their writing. Finally, the educators interrupted the presentation. "Yes, but where are your educational products? Don't you have any?"

The software producer, who was also a former public school teacher, tried to explain how his products would be useful in schools, how they had been tested, and were popular with teachers and their students.

The educators, however, protested. They said that creativity had been big in the '60s, but in the '80s they wanted software to help them manage. They wanted software that could show test scores. Since some parents were demanding a standard curriculum, they said they wanted computer software that would tell them where students were on that curriculum and help them control the system better.

The software producer tried to explain that computers were supposed to free teachers and students from drudgery. He tried to describe the research showing that many students learn more from tutoring by older students than from even the highest quality computer software.

The educators listened, clearly impatient and displeased. "So you can't make what we want. We'll go elsewhere."

* * *

One Sunday afternoon, a man phoned the father of several children his son went to school with. He knew that the second family had an extensive library of computer programs for young children. "We hear you know a lot about computers and that you have lots of stuff for little kids to do on computers," he said. "Would you mind if we copied your programs?" Told that the programs probably represented a fifteen-hundred-dollar investment, the man replied, "Oh, I'm not surprised. That's why I'd like to copy them." Asked whether he would ask to copy fifteen-hundred-dollars' worth of books, the caller said, "Well, I guess I hadn't thought about it that way." The family with the extensive program library offered to demonstrate the programs for the other family, and loaned them various computing magazines but refused permission to copy programs. The magazines came back that afternoon. The first family has not contacted the second family since.

* * *

The teacher had just walked around the conference center and was asking the software representative why so much of her company's material was the drill-and-practice variety. "Why aren't there more products that help students become more creative? Why isn't more available to help kids use the community? Why aren't any of the educational software producers coming up with new applications for computers? Why must we turn to the business people to develop ideas like word processing and database management? How about a little creativity from your industry?"

The woman looked at the teacher sadly. "Some of us are on your side and would like to do what you are describing. Some of us have made those arguments in corporate meetings. Do you know why we lose? Because companies know most schools won't buy that kind of material. A few years ago, I wrote a textbook for home economics. It was well reviewed. It encouraged students and their teachers to spend time in the community, doing comparison shopping. It suggested that students compare the quality of vegetables and produce in suburban and suburban supermakets. This was a challenging, creative textbook. But *it didn't sell*. It was blown away by textbooks that had students read some relatively boring material and answer questions at the end of each chapter. Teachers like that kind of textbook. They like that kind of software. Don't blame us for the kind of software that's available. Look at your profession. Will teachers support creativity? Will they accept materials that encourage going into the community? Will administrators support it? Will school boards?"

The teacher shrugged his shoulders, smiled sadly, and walked away.

*   *   *

National computer magazines are starting to report a new family problem that some experts call "Silicon Valley Syndrome." It often involves, according to Jean Hollands, a family counselor, "a marriage in which the male partner, usually an engineer or scientist, is over-involved in his work to the point of neglecting and thus endangering the marital relationship" (Bonner, p. 82). It seems that in some families, one person has become "addicted" to the computer. These people get up early in the morning to use the computer. They come home after work and disappear into the computer room and may not come out until the other partner is asleep.

*   *   *

A school district prided itself on its computer-managed instruction (CMI) program, for which it had received national attention. District educators wrote learning objectives in several curriculum areas. Then lessons were created for each objective. In math, students could be checked on whether they could add one-, two-, and three-digit numbers. In social studies, students could be tested to see whether they could name their states and capitals, and list the presidents. The CMI system stored all this information. It could instantaneously show what test a student had passed.

Some parents and teachers loved the system; others hated it. Supporters liked the precision. Detractors said that the district was reducing support for activities that were difficult to measure and record on computers: "What about creativity? What about artistic impression? Is this 'brave new world' we're going toward going to accelerate the disturbing trend toward treating art as irrelevant?" "Is human activity somehow less valuable if it can't be precisely measured and recorded on a computer?"

This district's answer to the last question appears to be yes. District priorities have been to continue and expand funding the CMI program. World languages, drama, music, and art have suffered significant budget cuts.

*   *   *

A group of five-year-olds were interviewed as they used their school's computers and the LOGO program to create various patterns. They were asked if doing this was more fun than drawing flowers or walking through a field with flowers. "God makes real flowers," explained one youngster. "These are only pretend. And the flowers in the field are prettier." Several other children said they like to do different things at different times. "Sometimes it's computer time, sometimes it's drawing time." What's the most fun, they were asked. The five-year-olds have a long list: "Playing with my cat, playing with 'He-man,' sleeping over at my friend's house, watching TV." "Doing something with my parents—that's the best," says a little boy. Several of the others agree quickly, "Yes, it's always more fun to do something with my parents." One youngster, who clearly would rather be working with the computer than talking to an adult, responds: "Playing with a computer is more fun than drawing or walking. The computer makes me feel like I'm God."

* * *

A group of self-described teenaged "computer hackers" were talking about why they like to spend so much time with the machines. Each of these young people, all of whom are white males from middle- to upper-income families, has a computer at home, and each claims to spend four to eight hours a day on the computer. They played a "can-you-top-this?" game for a while. One said, "My parents promised to take me on a trip to Hawaii if I'd cut down on the time on the computer. But I told them if we went to Hawaii, I'd just find some hackers there." Another reported, "My parents threatened to take the computer away if I didn't get some sleep. I agreed, but discovered they don't hear me if I get up early in the morning."

Why do they like computing? "It makes me feel powerful," answered one. The others laughed, but then agreed. "It's not so complicated. It's not hard, like asking a girl out. You are in control. You know that if you just work hard enough, you can figure out the problem. You don't have to depend on anyone else. It's totally up to you."

* * *

In these stories, computers hardly appear neutral. For the people involved, computers are influencing their lives, their careers, and their relationships. A machine as powerful as the personal computer cannot be neutral. It will alter our feelings about ourselves. It will change the way we communicate with others. It will influence the way we act. Just as people react differently to automobiles and television, they will not all view computers —or be affected by them—in the same way. Computers are having and will have an impact on our culture and society. We must not think only about what the computer can do *for* us; we must also consider what it is doing *to* us.

This question has been asked, but it's not yet getting the attention it deserves. In October 1980, members of the United States Congress studied the possible impact of computers and other advanced technology on American education. The House Committee on Education and Labor and two of its subcommittees asked the Congressional Office of Technology Assessment (OTA) to conduct a study of the subject. Two years later OTA published a report entitled *Informational Technology and Its Impact on American Education*. But while the report is two-hundred-and-sixty pages long, only one paragraph (itself only three sentences long) examines potential long-term problems that the extensive use of technology in education could produce.

Most schools don't teach much about the impact of technology on people. For example, television has been used much more that it has been studied. Television helps us make political and purchasing decisions. Television news is the major source of information about world events for half our population. Advertising helps create cultural norms. Both news and advertising influence the way we think.

Yet few students have ever visited a television studio or critically examined the process by which "news" is produced and edited. Few students have studied the techniques television advertisers use to encourage purchase of their product or service. It's very difficult to find an American school in which students are required to learn how television executives decide what programs will be put on the air, or what is done to shows to make them more attractive to viewers. Most nursery schools and day-care centers do not talk with young children about the connections between advertising and cartoon shows. The cultural stereotypes that are strengthened by advertising generally are ignored. Students are not encouraged to examine the ways blacks, Hispanics, Poles, Italians, and Native Americans (to mention a few groups) are portrayed on television.

Some of the best research and thinking about the potential impact of computers on human thought and action has been done by M.I.T. professor Sherry Turkle in *The Second Self: Computers and the Human Spirit*, a rich, important book that's impossible to summarize in a few paragraphs. Turkle spent six years interviewing people throughout the country who used computers extensively. In her book, she reports on how children look at computers in different ways, depending on their age and their level of maturity. She describes how computers fit into a very old debate regarding what are the essential qualities of being human. Her conclusion is worth quoting:

The riddle of mind . . . has taken on new urgency. Under pressure from the computer, the question of mind in relation to machine is becoming a central cultural preoccupation. It is becoming for us what sex was to the Victorians—threat and obsession, taboo and fascination (Turkle, p. 312).

Building on Turkle's work forces us to consider ways in which computers might change society. What problems could be created?

The *first* potential problem with computers is that they may encourage schools to concentrate on the kind of learning and teaching that is easily measured by machines. Computers can determine the number of mathematical mistakes a students makes and can even simulate the engineering details of a building. Computers can also detect the number of spelling, punctuation, and grammatical errors a student makes. But computers cannot measure the creativity or logic that a student uses in writing an essay.

It's entirely possible that the kind of learning a computer *can monitor* will become more important. It's also quite possible that the educational system will be modified to fit computer capability, rather than human needs. Learning could become more standardized, rather than individualized. Districts could continue the search for information *everyone needs to know*, and purchase computer programs promising to teach this. This standardization could triumph over the recognition that people learn in different ways.

An increasing number of parents want their children to develop strong skills and competencies. But parents also want opportunities to choose from among programs that develop those skills in various ways. When choices are offered, parents respond positively. Choice and competence are not incompatible. It would be tragic if computers were used to limit, rather than expand, choice.

A *second* problem with computers could be that they will retard human development. A computer can be used to draw a picture of a tree, grass, an ocean, or a rose. But it cannot replace the impact of smelling a real rose. Computers can't measure the beauty or ugliness of a building. They cannot substitute for the experience of lying on a beach, building a sand castle, and gazing at the ocean. Drawing a picture of a sandbox is one thing; playing in the sand is another. Child psychologists say young children need the opportunity to experience different textures, to smell, feel, taste, and touch. A lemonade-stand simulation game cannot replace the experience of setting up your own stand, deciding how much lemonade to make, and enjoying conversations with people who stop by to talk and buy your product. A fishing simulation game cannot replace the companionship of a family fishing trip. Playing an adventure game on a computer cannot replace climbing, jumping, sliding, and swinging at a playground or in a forest. If homes and schools become places where simulation is substituted for experience, our children and our society could lose sensitivity, creativity, insight, and vision.

Unquestionably, computers can help people experience things that they might otherwise never understand. A well-designed simulation game can help youngsters understand some of the challenges faced by pioneers who were trying to get from Missouri to Oregon in the 1840s. The best simulations can be used in conjunction with other activities to help learners get a better perspective on themselves and others.

Computer simulations can also save time and money. Some airlines use simulations to help train pilots. They learn to maneuver in various situations and become familiar with different airports long before actually flying. The lesson here is that we ought to consider when simulations are appropriate and valuable, and when they are limiting.

A *third* potential problem is that definitions of acceptable behavior may change. As mentioned earlier, some people think nothing of copying thousands of dollars' worth of computer programs. Some people feel that computer companies are not justified in charging the huge sums they do for programs. They try to defend their actions on the basis of "getting even with companies that are ripping off consumers." Many companies indeed charge too much, but will copying make programs less expensive? Some people who would never steal a product from a store are now, in effect, stealing computer programs. The subject is an intensely debated, unresolved topic at most computing conferences.

Our son and daughter, now six years old, are learning that it is not right to take someone else's property without their permission. That is theft. It is not acceptable to borrow a bicycle or a model spaceship without getting approval from the owner. Our son and daughter are also learning that it is not acceptable to copy a product someone bought, without the producer's permission. It is not acceptable to copy someone else's computer program. We will show people what we have, but not permit them to copy the programs. If our children see a program at school or in someone else's home that they think is worth obtaining, they should let us know. We'll try to get it, either at a library or in a computer store. And our children know their parents follow these same rules. They've heard conversations on this subject involving their parents and other computer users.

Children learn a great deal by watching adults. They are interested in what adults say, but generally more interested in what adults do. Copying computer disks ought to be unacceptable. It isn't enough to say this— we must live by that standard. Unfortunately, many people are changing their definitions of right and wrong, spurred on by the computer's power to permit quiet theft in their own homes. Like the legendary apple in the Garden of Eden, computing power is too strong for some people to resist.

A *fourth* potential problem is in the way computers may encourage people to think about problems. Programming is an extremely linear way of thinking. It has its own internal logic, which demands no human interaction. Thus, creating a box using the LOGO language requires a series of short, concrete, related steps. Here is the Logo sequence you would type into the computer to create a box:

FD 15. (This tells the machine to draw a line 15 spaces long.)

R 90. (This tells the machine to turn the "line drawer" 90 degrees to the right.)

FD 15. (This tells the machine to draw a line 15 spaces long that is perpendicular to the first line.)

R 90. (This tells the machine to turn the line 90 degrees to the right.)

FD 15. (The machine draws another line 15 spaces long, parallel to the original line and perpendicular to the second line.)

R 90. (The machine turns the line one last time, back toward the original line.)

FD 15. (The machine draws a fourth 15-space line, connecting the third line with the original, and creating a square.)

But human communication is more complicated than this list of isolated, lifeless steps makes it out to be. Progress requires discussion and negotiation. Human decisions often benefit from compromise and humor. But the computer's kind of reasoning has no use for such values. Programming a computer does not necessarily teach people how to get along better with each other. Computer programming may make people more impatient with other folks. Computers may encourage some people to withdraw from others, into their own powerful, hyper-rational world. As one fourteen-year-old boy explained, "If only girls were as easy to understand as computers!"

Of course, balancing the potential problems that computers may cause in our society are potential contributions. It's an ironic paradox that the computer—a powerful machine—may encourage us to make better use of our human capabilities. Teachers who have used word processing with students talk about how the computer changed—and improved—their relationships with students. They were able to spend much more time talking with students about major improvements in writing. And students had more interest in, and enthusiasm for, thinking about what they wanted to express because the computer made the mechanical progress of writing those ideas so much easier.

Computers have also already changed the lives of many handicapped persons. Some disabled people are now able to communicate with others, perform tasks, and assume responsibilities—actions that were impossible before the computer. Just as rockets have taken people places we only dreamed about thirty years ago, so computers have taken some handicapped people places that were only a vision five years ago.

Serious ethical problems and important creative contributions—these are hardly the characteristics of a *neutral* tool. Computers would seem to be anything but neutral in their effects on us and our society. We need to make certain that our children study what those effects are and not just how to use computers. The next chapter considers what children actually learn about computers. It examines the vague and increasingly popular notion of computer literacy.

MYTH 2: There is such a thing as
computer literacy, and every graduate of
our schools needs to have it.

4

COMPUTER LITERACY

The ability to use and understand computing is becoming as important as our ability to understand and handle
the written word. A computer-literate populace is as
necessary to an information society as raw materials and
energy are to an industrial society.

—Dorothy K. Deringer
and Andrew R. Molnar,
National Science Foundation, 1982

The next myth to be examined is this: "Computer literacy exists and every graduate of our schools needs to
have it." Readers may be surprised to learn that not only
do some authorities disagree with this statement, but
even those who agree with it differ in how they define
computer literacy.

At this point, however, your eyes may start to glaze
over: "Oh gosh, another silly argument among college
professors. There are probably ten people in the country who understand the debate—and another ten who
think it really matters." But before deciding that,
remember that state legislatures, boards of education,
and colleges are adopting requirements. Textbook companies are rushing materials into print to help teach the
subject. And so the controversy is much more than an

academic one—millions of dollars are being spent (and perhaps misspent) while the experts argue. For an increasing number of people, these various views are worth reviewing, understanding, and evaluating.

There are two different sorts of divisions in the field. The first division is between those who believe that all students should be required to know something about computers, and those who disagree. Those who favor some kind of computer literacy requirement, however, disagree about what computer literacy is. Some experts urge that all students should learn to *program* a computer—learn to give it a set of formal directions. Others recommend a broader definition: for them computer literacy means the knowledge of some programming, of potential applications of computers (such as word processing, spreadsheet analysis, and database management), and of the impact of the computer on society.

That there are different definitions of computer literacy hardly needs arguing. The following are only a few examples of diverse educational materials presently available to and being purchased by educators. All purport to offer instruction in computer literacy.

- *Basic Computer Literacy, Inc.*, of Manteno, Illinois, publishes a workbook and set of floppy disks geared to students grades six to eight. The materials describe different kinds of computers, the role of computers in our lives, how computers work, and different kinds of software, and then they provide an introduction to programming in BASIC, one of the most widely used computer languages.
- *International Business Machines* (IBM) has a much broader definition of computer literacy. In its Fall 1984 *IBM Personal Computer Educational Software Directory*, the corporation lists 128 different computer literacy products, offering instruction in typing; learning to write programs in computer languages like BASIC, LOGO, FORTRAN, Pascal, and FORTH; word processing; using spreadsheets and database management

programs to manipulate numbers, perform calcula-
tions, and organize information; problem-solving;
and communication with other computers.

- *Computer Literacy—A Hands-On Approach* is the single
most widely used text on this subject. The authors
devote ninety percent of their attention to teaching
students who use the book how to program a computer in BASIC, and then provide discussions of computer applications and the role of computers in
society.
- *Minnesota Educational Computing Corporation* (MECC)
provides a variety of products under the label of computer literacy. One, geared to elementary school children, introduces them to the computer keyboard,
computer terminology, graphics capability, and the
ability to save and access information. Other MECC
products in this general area include products to help
students learn to program and use various
applications.

Remember that these are just a few of the packages
available. In fact, a 1982 nationwide survey found that
there were more than 200 different software packages
available on the subject of computer literacy. Only one
package was being used by as many as five percent of
the schools (Anderson, 1983, p. 2). The intent here is not
to criticize these companies for the diversity of materials available. They are in a difficult spot, and they must
produce materials for a diverse market. It is clear, however, that no consensus exists about what computer literacy is. Both sides put forth arguments for their
definitions, and we will briefly examine each argument
below.

DOES COMPUTER LITERACY =
THE ABILITY TO PROGRAM A COMPUTER?
One nationally published textbook insists that people
who have the ability to program will know two important things: "What things a computer can do and how to

tell a computer to do the things *you* want it to do" (Luerhrmann and Peckham, p. 1). The authors are strong advocates of the programming approach to computer literacy, and Luerhrmann gives the following major arguments for it:

1. If students are not required to learn computer programming, many of them won't. National studies show that students who tend to take programming are white males of above-average intelligence, from above-average income families. Students who tend not to take programming are women, people of color (blacks, Hispanics, and Native Americans) and those from low-income families.

2. Computing is like mathematics. If offered the choice between learning mathematic applications (balancing a checkbook, figuring mileage, etc.) and algebra, most people will choose the most accessible and understandable applications. However, algebra is a foundation for many other courses, and, without realizing it, students limit their options by avoiding the subject.

3. Permitting students to avoid a programming class will limit their career options. Many high-paying jobs will require programming skills. Lower-paying jobs will require computer application skills (word processing, spreadsheet analysis, and database management).

National surveys do show that a vast majority of computers in secondary schools are being used to teach programming. A major national report by the National Science Board Commission on Precollege Education, *Educating for the 21st Century*, appears to support Luerhrmann. It recommends introducing computer literacy requirements (without clearly defining the term) for all teachers and then recommends requiring at least a one-semester course in computer science for high school graduation. Most computer science courses stress programming skills.

But an increasing number of people wonder whether students who have learned to program in one of the computer languages, such as BASIC or LOGO, and know a bit about the role of computers in the world are really free "from having to depend on and trust a computer expert," as Luerhrmann and Peckham promise they will be.

DOES COMPUTER LITERACY = THE ABILITY TO USE WORD PROCESSING AND SPREADSHEETS?

The executive editor of one of the largest computing magazines in the nation, *Personal Computing*, questions the notion that programming is a basic skill.

> Although learning how to program can be an extremely valuable skill—ask a few of the millionaires the computer industry has created in the last couple of years— most people simply do not need to write their own programs nor could they possibly profit directly from doing so (Fawcette, p. 183).

The editor goes on to urge helping people learn to use various computer applications. Gil Valdez of Minnesota's Department of Education strongly agrees with the application approach: "We just don't need that many programmers, but we need people who know how to use the machine to solve problems."

The most well-known of the recent national commissions on improving education supports the notion of the computer as a tool. The President's Commission on Excellence in Education recommended that before graduating each student complete a half-year course in computer science. This course should equip graduates to

> understand the computer as an information, computation, and communication device; use the computer in the study of the other basics for personal and work-related purposes; and understand the world of computers, electronics, and related technologies (National Commission on Excellence in Education, p. 26).

One writer's broad definition of computer literacy includes four basic abilities:

1. The ability to control and program a computer to achieve a variety of personal, academic, and professional goals.
2. The ability to use a variety of pre-programmed computer applications in personal, academic, and professional contexts.
3. The ability to make use of ideas from the cultures surrounding computer programming and computer applications as part of an individual's collection of strategies for information retrieval, communication, and problem solving.
4. The ability to understand the growing economic, social, and psychologicial impact of computers on individuals and groups within our society and on society as a whole (Watt, pp. 57-58).

Some of the best long-range thinking about this issue has been done by Marc Tucker, the director of the Carnegie Corporation's Forum on Education and the Economy. Tucker says that educators should be thinking about our future and helping to prepare thoughtful, skilled students to function successfully in it. He hopes for a future in which virtually all workers will be able to analyze and solve problems. To make that future possible, schools should use computers and other advanced technology to develop young people's communication, thinking, and analytic skills.

Don Rawitsch, a former classroom teacher who is now the director of user services for the Minnesota Educational Computing Corporation, agrees that it is silly to think that any person will be able to understand everything worth knowing about computers by taking a single course. He suggests that computer literacy include several components, including controlling computers, using applications, and understanding their social impact. He questions the value of a mandated, centrally developed course called "computer literacy" and instead urges that each district or school determine its own definition "based on local decisions and priorities."

Rawitsch's views are supported by Budd and Delores Hagen, two parents who've worked with handicapped and disabled people throughout North America. They think that people need to learn to use computers to make their lives easier and more fulfilled. For some people, that will involve a mastery of one, two, or three computer languages. But the Hagens are convinced that most people don't need to know programming. Budd Hagen says that requiring whoever uses a computer to learn programming is like "requiring everyone who wants a driver's license to know how to take apart and rebuild an engine."

Delores Hagen agrees. She works with people who are just learning that they can communicate with others. "Many disabled or handicapped people have almost given up on life. Problem-solving via programming is so far from where they are at that the term is truly a joke. Someday they may learn to program, and that will be fine. In the meantime, we want them to learn to type, and use word processing and other computer applications." She concludes, "To devote so much time, attention, and money to teaching programming to teachers and students—what a mistake!"

Having examined the term "computer literacy" and discovered that it means different things to different people, we can now look at the second part of the myth under consideration: every graduate of our schools needs to have computer literacy (whatever your definition of it is).

The debate over this question is heated and vigorous. Nationally, it appears that the pressure is increasing for schools to teach their students *something* about computers. A 1984 Gallup Poll reports that sixty-eight percent of the public believes that some kind of computer training should be required (up from forty-three percent in 1981) (Gallup, p. 31).

As we've seen, large, powerful corporations are creating materials to support the notion that some kind of computer literacy should be required. They are in business, after all, to make money selling computers and educational materials, and so they will use ingenuity, hype, and guilt to convince parents, educators, and others that their products are worth buying.

Other authorities, however, insist that we don't have enough qualified teachers or know enough about the impact or value of computers to require everyone to study them. One such authority, Joseph Weizenbaum, a professor of computer science at M.I.T., is deeply disdainful of the computer literacy concept, which he calls "the current version of body odor." For several thousand years, he explains, people did not worry about body odor. They took care of it with soap and water, or they ignored it. Then pharmaceutical companies invented deodorant and created the notion of body odor to sell their product. The professor believes that computer illiteracy is comparable.

> Someone has invented a brand new mental disorder, "computer illiteracy," and it's very dangerous and parents are convinced that their children will really be horribly disadvantaged if they aren't inoculated against this terrible disease. I would think it a joke if it weren't so sad (Weizenbaum, p. 96).

While rejecting the notion of computer literacy, Weizenbaum is not opposed to the use of computers in schools. He thinks it makes sense to use them in certain situations, such as word processing, but objects to requiring everyone to use the machine.

WHAT'S HAPPENING IN THE SCHOOLS

No one is surprised to learn that the diversity of opinion among scholars and corporations regarding computer literacy is reflected in school programs. Some school districts have no computer literacy requirement; others do. And there is absolutely no consensus among school people about what should be taught.

All eighth-grade Hartford, Connecticut, students take a twenty-five hour computer literacy course because the school district thinks that students must become knowledgeable about computers. The required course covers information about what a computer can do, the possible social implications of computers, and fundamental concepts of various programming languages. "We are not out to make everyone a master programmer," explains George Haddad, the district's computer coordinator. "We think it's much more important that students know about the impact and abilities of computers. But we also want students to understand the basic principles of programming." Haddad believes it's important for people who get an incorrect computer-generated bill to understand that the problem was not necessarily with the computer, but with the person who fed information into the machine. "We want our students to understand how people direct the machines." For the present, Haddad is satisfied that eighth grade is the right time for the computer literacy course. "Students seem enthusiastic, and parents say they want their children to learn about computers."

New York City faces a challenge different from most places. Its nearly one million students attend one thousand schools in thirty-seven separate, autonomous districts, all of which report to the chancellor of education. Mike Ryan, director of the city's Computer and Information Science Unit, says that the districts experimented several years ago with a computer literacy approach. "At that time [1983] we had very few computers, so we developed materials that did not require computers. But the word came back from the districts that 'computer literacy' was a bad term. People want to see students 'computer comfortable.'" The city has since purchased thousands of computers—about 6,000 by mid-1984—and it has de-emphasized the teaching of programming. Ryan reports, "We want kids to understand ways they can use computers. So we train them at the elementary and middle school levels in word processing. There is a brief introduction to programming in the early years, and the opportunity to go more deeply into a particular computer language in high school."

Fifteen hundred miles away, the state of Texas has decided to require a somewhat similar course. By the 1985-1986 school year, each of the state's eleven hundred districts must schedule either its seventh or its eighth grade into one-semester, half-hour computer literacy courses. The class will cover terminology, computer history, applications, programming, and the impact of computer use in society.

In a 1984 survey, the national educational computing magazine *Electronic Learning* found that twenty states and the District of Columbia had developed some kind of computer literacy mandate for their students. In some cases, the requirements will begin immediately. In others, they will be delayed for several years to permit time to develop the curriculum. Requirements took the following forms:

- Each student must have taken a class in computing before graduating: Indiana, Louisiana, New Hampshire, South Dakota, Tennessee, Utah, Wisconsin.
- Each student must have computer literacy skills before graduating: District of Columbia, Rhode Island, Texas, Virginia.
- Students must have computer experience in some course(s) before graduating: Florida, Hawaii.
- Students must choose from among several courses before graduation, one of which is computer literacy: Georgia.
- Students must be exposed to information technology before graduating: Minnesota.
- All schools must either offer a computer course or integrate computers in their curriculum: New Mexico, North Carolina, Vermont.
- Schools must offer a course for grades nine through twelve that deals in part with typing or keyboarding skills: Ohio.

Given these requirements, it's intriguing to learn that only six states had any kind of mandated experience in computing for prospective teachers. Where will the instructors come from to teach these courses in public schools? Who will teach the prospective teachers? Can it be safely assumed that there are enough computer literate people in colleges to teach the undergraduates?

These questions must be considered in any definition, and in any decision to require things of young people. Why? Well, let's assume that many states decide in 1985 that all their students must be *rocket* literate— they must know how to build rockets. Assume also that this is a worthy goal. But most of the teachers now in the schools will not know much about building rockets: it's never been expected of them, and so most have not learned it. Are there enough people in colleges who know how to build rockets to teach all the prospective and present teachers who must be retrained? Finally, if only six states require that that college students training to be teachers must take courses in rocket building, where will the other fourteen states that have mandates about rocket-building courses for schools (not to mention the other thirty states that are trying to do something with rockets in their schools) get their teachers?

While states and schools are developing various policies, there may soon be strong pressure to standardize. The Education Testing Service (ETS) has a federal contract to conduct a National Assessment of Educational Progress. ETS is the corporation that developed and operates the College Entrance Examination Board, producer of one of the major college entrance tests in the country (Scholastic Aptitude Tests). This national assessment has been conducted periodically in the last decade, covering topics such as writing, math, citizenship, and science skills and knowledge. In the spring of 1986, the assessment will include questions about students' computer competence.

APPROPRIATE PUBLIC POLICY
AMID THE CONFUSION

It's not easy to decide whom to believe among the conflicting arguments over computer literacy. But resolution is important. As one educational computing expert explained, "Disagreements over what should be included within the definition of computer literacy have not only academic but curricular import" (Anderson, 1980, p. 13). Several assumptions can help guide people who care about these issues.

First, the technology will continue to change dramatically. Computers will become much easier to understand, will respond to voice rather than typed commands, and will be small enough to be carried in shirt pockets.

Second, new uses will be created for computers. New applications will evolve as people learn more about computer capabilities and use their creativity to take advantage of those capabilities.

Third, computers probably will play a growing role in many jobs. But while it's likely that more people will need to be familiar with the capabilities and limitations of computers, not everyone must feel comfortable with computers.

Fourth, people are much better at creating technology than using it well. This is not a criticism of technology itself, but a reminder of our human limitations.

Fifth, in our schools, few students study technology's impact on our lives. Driver education is a classic example. Students learn the "rules of the road" and how to operate the car, but there is virtually no discussion of funding for mass transit, the results of running freeways through neighborhoods, or alternatives to the automobile. With television, the situation is even worse. Very few *study* the television set. Oh, they watch it— thousands of hours. But few courses (and certainly almost no required courses) encourage and assist students to consider issues like how television commercials encourage consumption, how the news is gathered and edited, and how new programs are created.

Sixth, computers are unique technological tools; they are significantly different than mathematics, pencils, telephones, and automobiles—some of the tools with which they are metaphorically linked. These metaphors, however, are imprecise and inexact. As Don Rawitsch explains, the powerful people in the emerging society "will be those who control information, not transportation."

Seventh, there is a major problem training people qualified to teach about computers. Expertise in universities and school districts varies, as do opportunities to get access to high-quality training programs.

Eighth, training that's provided by people who have an economic interest in a particular machine or technology is unlikely to be neutral or comprehensive. These people have a legitimate view, but they are much too close to the situation to provide balanced, complete information.

Ninth, assessment of computing competence should include both paper-pencil and practical applications of computing. Some of the most important computing skills can be measured only with the use of a real computer.

Tenth, debates over the value and components of computer literacy are likely to continue in learned journals, on talk shows, and at conferences. Meanwhile, people in the schools will continue working with students, sorting through various arguments, and adapting part of what most experts say.

Most adults agree on the need for young people to be able to read, write, and calculate. These skills can be defined and measured. They can be used regardless of new or advancing technologies. But when machines are changing rapidly, becoming much easier to use, and developing new methods of operating, it is not appropriate to require that everyone understand how to give them a certain set of instructions. Instead of trying to develop a course on computer literacy, authorities should consider the following recommendations.

1. Any educational requirements about computers must be subject to change and modification.
2. Every child should learn about the ways technology affects our individual and societal thinking, feeling, and interacting. The potential social impact of computers as a topic should be a high priority.
3. Teaching all students to program in a particular language should *not* be a high priority.
4. Courses in programming a computer ought to be available, as are other vocational subjects, but should not be required.
5. Computers should be used throughout the school curriculum in places where their capabilities will ease, challenge, encourage, and motivate on a cost-effective basis.
6. Students should learn how to turn on machines and care for floppy disks and computers in elementary school. This instruction should be a preface to using the computer to accomplish a broader objective, such as using a simulation game or beginning to learn keyboard skills.
7. Educators should have opportunities to learn about computers from various institutions. This includes both universities and computing organizations, with university credit available for completion of courses at nontraditional institutions.
8. In general, training should be provided by people who are not employees of companies producing computers. Educators and parents need to get the broadest, fairest, and most comprehensive information possible, but they are unlikely to receive unbiased information from instructors employed by a particular company.

Authorities can save a great deal of time and money by avoiding the impulse to rush off toward a computer literate society. Concentrating resources on teaching programming and some kind of vaguely defined computer literacy course is neither wise nor appropriate public policy. Before deciding how to use computers to encourage learning, we ought to examine some of the research about their impact.

MYTH 3: Using computers is the most effective way for most students to learn most subjects.

5

NEW RESEARCH ABOUT COMPUTERS AND LEARNING

I believe that the computer presence will enable us to so modify the learning environment outside the classroom that much if not all the knowledge schools presently try to teach with such pain and expense and such limited success will be learned, as the child learns to talk, painlessly, successfully and without organized instruction.

—Seymour Papert,
Mindstorms, 1980

This chapter questions a rather sweeping assertion: using computers is the most effective way to teach most subjects to most students. Many educators accept this assertion, and are frustrated because good material is not available to teach their courses. But computers may not be the best way to teach everything. Perhaps our use of them should be more selective and sophisticated.

A review of some of the research that has been conducted measuring the impact of computers on learning will help us identify sense and nonsense about this particular myth. Investigations show that some of the most common uses of computers are the most ill-advised. In this chapter, I will take a look at a few of the studies that have been done. People generally write books to share their own opinions, and my purpose in doing this book is no exception. The summary of research that follows will be comforting to those who share my values, and provocative to those who disagree with them. However, no claim is being made that this is an unbiased review of research. Wise readers will use this summary, together with other information available, to reach their own conclusions.

PEOPLE CAN DO MANY THINGS BETTER THAN COMPUTERS CAN

There are many things people can do more effectively than computers. A recent study by Stanford University's Institute on Educational Finance and Governance supports this belief. Researchers compared the cost-efficiency of four proposed reforms for improving elementary students' reading and math skills. The four were reducing class size, using computer-assisted instruction, increasing the instructional time devoted to mathematics and reading, and employing cross-age tutoring. These strategies were adopted because they had been designed to improve students' skills, could be used by other school districts, supplemented other efforts to improve skills, and had been studied enough so that there was "sufficient statistical evidence for an acceptable evaluation" (Levin, p. 4).

The evaluators found that having upper elementary age students tutor younger students was "far more cost-effective than a widely used computer-assisted instruction approach" (Levin, p. 30). The computer-assisted instructional approach involved in the test is one of the most widely advertised and (in my opinion) well developed of those presently available. Tutoring was also found to be more cost-effective in teaching reading and mathematics than reducing class size or increasing the amount of time spent instructing students.

Some people find this conclusion hard to believe, but it is not really so surprising. Most of us respond better to someone working directly with us than to a machine. Most of us learn more in a small group than in a large one.

There is a long (but often ignored) history in this country of older students helping younger ones. This was one of the principal strategies employed in one-room schoolhouses. Many senior citizens recall how much they enjoyed the opportunity to be tutored, and later, the opportunity to do the tutoring of someone younger. These observations are not surprising to people who are aware of (or have worked in) youth tutoring-youth programs developed in some schools during the 1980s. Careful research reported in Alan Gartner's *Children Teach Children* found that both those receiving and those providing tutoring in math and reading showed significant academic gains. It makes sense. If you are going to teach someone, you must know the subject well.

No one is saying that students can teach other students the rules of chemistry or algebra better than a teacher or a well-designed computer program supplementing a teacher. But school districts thinking of investing thousands or even millions of dollars in computers and related software for elementary classes should consider the results of these studies. The districts might make much more efficient use of their resources by training upper elementary and junior high school students to spend an hour of their day working with younger students.

COMPUTERS WILL BE MORE
INTERESTING AND USEFUL
FOR SOME STUDENTS THAN OTHERS

Students respond to computers in different ways: some are entranced with computers, and some find them boring. Intriguing research shows that children learn in different ways. Equally important, they may learn in various ways about different things. For example, I would rather read a book about improving schools than listen to a lecture on the topic. But I much prefer hearing someone explain home repairs instead of trying to figure them out in a book. Drs. Kenneth and Rita Dunn have found that there are major differences in learning styles, which they classify in four groups:

Emotional. Some people are more motivated, persistent, and responsible than others. Some prefer a situation that is constantly and continuously monitored; others make more progress when given general directions and allowed to move ahead at their own pace.

Environmental. Students differ in the ways they react to the temperature, light, sound, and design of a learning environment.

Sociological. Some students do better working by themselves, others working in small groups, and others working with large groups.

Physical. Some students learn more in the morning, others in the afternoon; some have a short attention span while others can sit still for hours; some learn more by reading, others by listening, and others by experimenting (Dunn and Dunn, p. 33).

These findings have direct application for the use of computers in education. Recently, one thousand teachers from all over the country were asked about the impact of having a microcomputer in their class. Twenty-four percent of them said there was much more learning by above-average students. Seven percent said there was much more learning by below-average students. Six percent said there was much more learning by average students (*Electronic Learning*, September 1983, p. 18).

There are many possible interpretations of these results. Perhaps bright students were given more opportunities to use the computer than other students. Perhaps teachers did not know much about the computers, so students who could figure out the machine for themselves gained most from it. Perhaps the computer permitted bright students to move ahead much more quickly than the classroom structures permitted. One can speculate endlessly.

Other studies appear to contradict the finding that bright students learn more from computers than average or below-average students. Dr. M. D. Roblyer of Florida A & M University recently conducted a review of more than twenty-five major, carefully designed studies about the impact of computers on learning. She concluded that computer-based instruction is

- more effective at lower levels (elementary rather than secondary),
- more effective with remedial than with high-achieving students, and
- more useful as a supplement than as a replacement of the teacher.

She observed that computer-based education generally has shown itself to be only equal to, and sometimes less effective than, other nontraditional approaches (such as tutoring). Roblyer concluded that "the evidence of success is not overwhelming" for computer-based learning.

Roblyer's findings are confirmed in part by the investigations of Glen Fisher, a school computer specialist in Alameda County, California. Fisher says that computers are *least* effective

- when there is no teacher input,
- when attempts are made to replace teachers with computers,

- with reading and language arts (English) lessons, and
- with students of average ability.

Fisher's work also shows that "computer-assisted instruction is an effective use of computers for certain students, in some subject areas, as a supplementary activity." Computer-assisted instruction seems to be *most* effective

- with students of low or high ability,
- when it is used as part of an overall course supervised by a teacher, and
- when it is used in a science or foreign language course (Fisher, p. 84).

Another national study shows that some students gain much more from a course on programming computers than others do. In the 1977-78 school year, the National Assessment of Educational Progress surveyed approximately twenty-five hundred thirteen- and seventeen-year-olds from all over the country. Relatively few of the students reported they had taken a course in computer programming—just eleven percent of the seventeen-year-olds. But "about half of the students who had taken computer programming classes were still unable to read a simple flowchart"—a diagram describing how a program is written (Anderson, 1980, p. 14). There are many possible interpretations of the result. The quality of instruction may have varied. Students' interest and intelligence levels may have been quite different. Some of the programming courses may have lasted much longer than others. Nevertheless, a significant number of students who took a programming course did not learn one of the simple and most basic parts of programming.

Research on the impact of computers on the attitudes and achievements of handicapped students is much more encouraging. Frank Bowe, an author and consultant on issues concerning disabled and older persons, summarized, in late 1984, the studies on handicapped students using computers to learn. Bowe cites research by Marc Gold showing that when information is broken into small units, and each unit is taught separately (as a well designed computer program does), "retarded students learn things previously thought to be beyond their abilities" (Bowe, p. 123). Another study showed that severely retarded students, with IQs ranging from 30 to 88, could be taught the location and use of the keys on a computer keyboard (Loebl and Kantrov, p. 39).

An *Infoworld* magazine reporter found similar results when she talked with handicapped adults who were learning to use computers. The adults were physically handicapped, but there was nothing handicapped about their minds. Many of them talked about how they would probably be on welfare or in minimal-skill jobs if adjustments had not been made on computers. Now they can (and are) getting well-paid jobs as computer programmers (Watt, p. 30).

How can these findings be reconciled? Some say that bright students will gain more from computers, but others suggest that computers will have more impact on students who have experienced failure in the past. It seems fair to conclude that computers will not be of equal value to all students. Some people are intrigued by computers, others find them boring. Moreover, some students will be interested in word processing, while others are more attracted to programming.

We can draw several conclusions from the research just described:
1. In general, students will react differently to computers. Some students will be intrigued instantly and will tend to learn more than others by using them.
2. Providing opportunities to use computers in various ways will increase the number and range of students who gain from them. This means that devoting most or all of a school's computers to one or two functions is not a good idea.
3. It is not wise to think that computers will replace teachers. Just as the most effective teachers use field trips, books, magazines, outside speakers and other

resources to extend and enrich learning, so they will use computers.

WORD PROCESSING OFFERS PROMISE OF IMPROVING MANY STUDENTS' WRITING SKILLS

Many communities are trying to improve students' writing skills by using word-processing programs. Since the earliest attempts to do this in elementary or secondary schools seem to have started about 1982, little formal research exists as yet. As of early 1985, two kinds of research had been reported.

An example of the first kind comes from the high school in Lakeville, Minnesota. For several years, students in some courses have been using word processing to help with their writing. As part of his work for an advanced degree, teacher Ed Mako compared students who used word processing with those who did not. The two groups represented both sexes and various levels of ability. His first finding was that those using word processing wrote significantly more than the control group as they moved from rough draft to final copy. Mako's second finding was that the group using word processing made almost twice as many major changes in their essays as did the students who were not using computers. His third finding was that it took less time for teachers to comment on the computer-using students' papers, partly because the computer-printed essays were much easier to read. Mako's research helped convince the local school board and building principal that the high school should have a computer lab devoted exclusively to word processing.

Another study compared two classes of third and fourth graders. One group spent four months working with a word-processing program designed especially for young children. The second group had only normal writing experiences. Papers from both groups were compared at the beginning and the end of the four-month period. Investigators analyzed writing samples for number of words and overall quality (as measured by adherence to topic and organization). The elementary students using word processing increased the number of words in their essays by sixty-four percent while there was no increase in the other class. In addition, the young people using word processing made a dramatic improvement in quality ratings, while the other group did not (Greenfield, pp. 141-42).

The second kind of research about word processing is anecdotal: teachers describing how the introduction of word processing increased students' interest in, and enthusiasm for, writing. An article by three Bloomfield, New Jersey, educators, two of whom are elementary school teachers, is a good example of this sort of evidence. After a year of using a computer in their classrooms, the teachers were pleased. Eighty percent of their sixth-grade students wanted to continue using word processing. Seventy-five percent of the students said writing was easy or enjoyable. The students' comments about word processing may be even more interesting than the statistics. Students described word processing as "using the computer for something other than shooting down aliens; changing a paragraph without doing the whole thing over again, helping you become a better reader, speller and editor; putting the good ideas in your brain into the computers; and having fun writing when you get the hang of it" (Palmer et al, p. 45).

A New York City teacher reported progress when she brought a computer into her English classes. She expected and found that "students who already wrote well, and who had found their own 'voice,' loved writing with the computer and quickly learned to use it." What she didn't expect was that "some of the weakest students in the class were unusually insistent about having their turn at writing with the computer. . . . Much to my surprise and delight, I began to notice a remarkable change in these students. Where there had been negativity, unreachability and a disturbing lack of purpose, I began to notice signs of competence and growth" (O'Brien, p. 20).

USE OF COMPUTERS
HAS POTENTIALLY NEGATIVE
AS WELL AS POSITIVE CONSEQUENCES

A mystique that must be monitored closely is developing about computers. Computers, like other machines, sometimes have problems, yet the Minnesota Educational Computing Corporation found that many students blame themselves for the machines' problems. Problems with a machine may influence a student's attitude for some time. In a Minnesota experiment, more than 350 secondary students using computers worked on a twenty- to thirty-minute science unit concerning water pollution. A computer breakdown, deliberately created by the researchers, occurred for some of the students. Students were asked which of the following they thought caused the breakdown:
• something in the computer system,
• something you did or didn't do, or
• some combination of the computer system and you.
The results:
• Forty-two percent of the students blamed themselves,
• Twenty-six percent blamed the computer, and
• Thirty-two percent blamed both the computer and themselves.

Thus, almost seventy-five percent of the students said they bore some responsibility for the problem. In fact, they had nothing to do with the malfunction. Equally important, this incident influenced students' views for at least six months; they were more likely than other students to think that their computers would break down.

Another study showed that student encounters with computers will not necessarily be positive. Carnegie-Mellon University in Pittsburgh recently adopted a requirement that all students learn to program a computer. Some students find programming to be extremely difficult and frustrating. Three professors learned that "most liberal arts students held a negative view of their required encounter with computer programming. . . . Students often were confused, angry and discouraged by trying to master computer programming. . . . Students in computing were very angry, as much as four times more frequently than in other courses" (Sproull et al., 1984).

One series of studies showed the importance of the physical setting in which computers are located. Much more investigation of this issue has been done by business than educational researchers. Corporations have learned that "the user's need for proper lighting is of paramount importance. . . . Improper lighting causes problems such as eyestrain, headaches and muscle strains because the user is forced to assume uncomfortable and awkward seating positions to see the video screen" (Cutler, p. 82). Another major issue is the kind of furniture used in a classroom. Several studies found that furniture designed specifically for use with computers increased corporate productivity by as much as fifteen percent. This means that school boards and parents should get informed advice about lighting, seating, and the height of computers. They should not just buy computers and put them on desks in a room.

WHAT DOES ALL THIS MEAN?

Many people believe that it is possible to find a study that proves almost anything. And there are some topics for which that is true. Research is available to show that flunking students is a good idea and a bad idea, that parental involvement in schools makes no difference and makes a big difference, and that more money spent on education has little effect or great impact. But conflicting findings don't necessarily negate the research. Lots of money has already been spent investigating the impact of computers on learning. Many people who are unsure about how to use computers in schools and homes will find the research useful.

From my perspective, there are a number of important conclusions to be drawn from this research:

1. People can do some things better than computers.
2. Computers will be more interesting and useful to some students than to others.
3. Taking a course about computing does not necessarily mean a student will learn much about the subject. Requiring that students master programming does not guarantee that they will have a positive experience.
4. Some people are intimidated by complex machines. Unless steps are taken to ensure that the limitations as well as the capabilities of machines are clear, some people will blame themselves for mistakes made by others.
5. Word processing has the potential to dramatically improve both students' attitudes and their ability to write.
6. Sophisticated uses of computers will enable handicapped people to gain skills and assume responsibilities previously viewed as not possible.
7. If a person's initial experiences with computers are positive, the person is much more likely to want to learn more about and with the machines.
8. The physical setting of rooms where computers are used will have a significant impact on students' performances and comfort. Educators and parents should examine research from the corporate world about proper furniture and lighting for rooms where computers are being used.

We should not accept the generalization that using computers is the most effective way to teach most subjects. It's more accurate to say that using computers *can* be an effective way to increase learning for *some* students in *some* subjects.

MYTH 4: Computers will revolutionize our schools.

6

COMPUTERS ENTER REAL SCHOOLS

The so-called information revolution, driven by rapid advances in communication and computer technology, is profoundly affecting American education. It is changing the nature of what needs to be learned, who needs to learn it, who will provide it, and how it will be provided and paid for.

—John H. Gibbons, Director,
U.S. Congress Office
of Technology Assessment, 1982

Despite the widespread belief that "computers will revolutionize schools," they aren't quite doing that. Most schools haven't changed their basic organizational patterns, curriculum goals, or instructional practices to reflect changing needs and opportunities. Most schools still have students of the same age sitting together in classrooms, with certified teachers leading the classes. Most class assignments are the same for each student. The emphasis is still on recalling the facts, opinions, and concepts the teacher finds appropriate. And many people think this is the way it should be.

Computers provide new possibilities, and some experts think the "information revolution" ought to encourage schools to act in fundamentally different ways. But most schools have made only minor modifications because of computers. Unless parents, teachers, and school board members have a clear understanding of alternative arrangements, things will go on pretty much as they have been. Another opportunity to improve our schools and increase the number and percentage of youngsters who gain basic and applied skills will have been wasted.

For many reasons, computers haven't come close to achieving their potential. Unless significant action is taken soon, computers will follow the pattern set by other technological advances: they will have an enormous impact on our *society*, but little impact on our *schools*.

Who decides how many computers a school will have? Who decides which teachers and students will use them, and for what purposes? How do teachers find out about exciting things happening in other schools? How do students hear about computers? What can parents do to influence things? What can be done to encourage talented teachers to stay in the classroom, and to encourage bright young people to enter the teaching profession? Most people have no answers to these questions. Yet, if progress is to be made, there must be greater understanding of such issues.

In this chapter, I want to examine the case history of one urban school that decided, in 1978, to use computers. Research shows that this school's experience is typical of the vast majority of the programs in the nation. Considering the challenges and dilemmas it faced will illustrate "the real world of public schools." Recommendations and suggestions about computer use must take into account the particular situations in which educators and parents find themselves.

The school under consideration was a junior high school in St. Paul, Minnesota. In the mid-1970s, it had two computer terminals, linked by telephone lines to the state's computer system. The terminals were used occasionally by a few students, and eventually by school administrators for student registration.

In 1978, one of the administrators and a math teacher submitted a request for personal computers for the school, and two were purchased. The math teacher knew a bit about computer programming, and he worked with several students interested in it. After a year of experimentation, he offered a course on programming as an elective in the math department. Most of the students who took it were white males who excelled in mathematics.

In 1979, a new math teacher, enthusiatic about computers, joined the staff and requested a few more computers. Other staff members became interested in experimenting with the computers, and the school purchased some software.

Then, with a grant from the federal government, the school was able to buy eight more computers. A formal course on programming was offered to the students, and approximately 120 (more than twenty-five percent of the student body) signed up for it.

Part of the federal grant was used to establish a program for students who were not doing well in school. With the help of the school district's computer coordinator, teachers bought software that drilled students on math and reading. Some of the software permitted students to race horses or shoot at aliens if they answered the questions quickly and accurately. It was popular with some of the students, who said it was "much better than the dumb textbooks." In all, some of the students enjoyed using the computer, while others quickly lost interest. (This latter group much preferred working in a room with a teacher who came around to students.)

By 1981, the school was moving ahead with its use of computers, involving more staff and providing students with more exposure to its machines. The school sponsored several well-received events. A one-day workshop for faculty members, for example, kindled interest among English, foreign language, science, and music teachers for using computers in their particular subject areas. Also, a computer fair, with displays by local computer stores and student demonstrations of computer uses, generated excellent community response. And a well-received program describing careers in computing was attended by students from throughout the school district.

Because of its success, some of the details of what happened at the workshop are worth reporting. The school invited all of its twenty teachers to a Saturday workshop; eighteen attended, plus about six other teachers from nearby programs. Since no local university professor appeared to have extensive, comprehensive experience working with schools, the school hired a staff member from the Minnesota Educational Computing Corporation (MECC) to lead the group. She brought in a range of programs including word processing, drill and practice, games, and supplementary material.

A successful educational computing workshop, the teachers concluded, had the following characteristics:

- It allowed teachers to learn enough to actually use a program. Teachers feared they might not be able to do much at the first session but were delighted to discover that it look less than fifteen minutes to learn how to turn a computer on and off and insert a "floppy disk" containing the program. As one teacher commented, "this workshop really 'demystified' computers for me." Another wrote that the workshop leader's attitude was that "she was there to be helpful, not to convince us that computers are very complicated. She made me feel smart, not stupid."
- It let teachers try out various programs relevant to their courses.
- It provided enough computers so that they had to share with only one other person.
- It was led by someone who could answer specific, critical questions about classroom applications.

- It was set up by administrators who were willing to work out a cooperative plan to use computers in the school, rather than have one imposed from the central or principal's office.
- It provided followup sessions. Many people were using small computers for the first time. A number of teachers wrote that there was only so much information they could absorb in one day.

Despite the success of these kinds of events, there were also problems connected with computer use in the school. For the sake of security, the administration placed most of the computers in a central location—next to the math teacher's classroom—that seriously restricted other teachers' access to them. Some teachers, who were highly enthusiastic about computers, moved on to other schools or positions, so their expertise was lost. And the school's administrators changed frequently.

It was also difficult for teachers to get permission from the district to attend outside workshops. In this district, as in many others, it was considered a privilege to attend outside workshops, not a right. One teacher's request to attend such a workshop was denied by an office administrator who doubted that the district would get much benefit from the teacher's attendance. The teacher took the denial philosophically. "Well, we tried," he said. "But there is a difference in the district's attitude toward teachers and administrators, isn't there? They see us [the teachers] more like little children who are trying to figure out ways to cheat and slough off. And sometimes it's hard to avoid a self-fulfilling prophecy—people begin to act the way others expect them to act." Fortunately, this teacher is an extremely hardworking and conscientious person. Though disappointed, he continued to provide leadership and assistance to students and other faculty in the building.

The story continues. By early 1985, the school had one computer for every twenty-five students. Administrators were using computers to keep records and assist with the scheduling of classes. A number of students were learning to program computers, using either BASIC or LOGO. Special education students were working with a computer, primarily on reading, English, and mathematics problems. Two teachers with an interest in word processing had been named administrators.

It would be hard to demonstrate that this public school was a fundamentally different place than it had been five years before. The school had bought more than thirty thousand dollars' worth of machines and perhaps an additional five thousand dollars' worth of software. Several thousand dollars' worth of training had been provided. The school had had a good reputation before it started using computers, and retained a good reputation in 1985.

But was the education substantially different, substantially better because of computers? Student achievement test scores were not significantly higher. Students' attitudes toward themselves, school, and learning had not improved significantly. The morale of the teachers had not increased dramatically. There was no evidence that parents were much more satisfied with the education their children were receiving than parents had been five years earlier. There was little objective evidence to say that computers had had a major impact on learning or teaching at this school. After five years, extraordinary results are hard to find.

As an administrator involved for several years with this particular school, I was both a participant in, and observer of, the process. While gathering information for this book, I visited more than a hundred schools around the country, and it's clear that this case history is not unusual—there are many schools with similar histories. Scholars at Johns Hopkins University studied patterns of computer use at more than 1,000 secondary schools around the nation between December 1982 and February 1983 (Becker, pp. 41-44). Most of the following generalizations, gleaned from that research, were also true of our school sample.

- Teaching programming and using drill-and-practice software were the two most common ways that secondary schools used computers.
- Students learning about programming tended to be white males from middle- and above-average-income families; they also tended to be doing well in school.
- The computer language used to teach programming was BASIC.
- Students using the drill-and-practice, remedial software tended to be those who were not doing well in school, often black and Hispanic students from middle- and low-income families.
- Most secondary schools using computers had at least one teacher, often a mathematics instructor, who was considered the resident computer expert.
- In about half the schools studied, only one or two teachers, at most, regularly used the computer. (This was true at the sample school until about 1983, when several other teachers started using computers with their classes.)
- School computers were used an average of 2.5 hours a day. This meant that computers were not turned on more than half of the six-hour school day. (By contrast, at the sample school, eighty to ninety percent of the computers were on from half an hour before school started to an hour after classes ended.)
- There were about five computers for the average secondary school of 700. (Again, by contrast, at the sample school there were fourteen computers serving the 480 students.)
- About thirteen percent of the students at the average secondary school were able to use the computer during the week. (At the sample school, more than twenty-five percent of the students were using the computer.)

People who think that computers will revolutionize education must understand the challenges and dilemmas that exist in public schools. Scholars, legislators, and professional educators are beginning to understand that our system of public education often discourages and then absorbs innovation. Someone compared the public school system to a pillow. You push, and it gives way a bit. But when you look at it after a while, it's back in almost the same shape it was before. Many schools are not changing their overall instructional methods, their instructional goals, their personnel policies, or their relationships with communities to reflect computer capabilities. They are simply adding a few requirements—a course here, a unit there. Computers will have relatively little impact unless other changes occur along with their introduction.

7

LEARNING FROM THE PAST/ LESSONS FOR THE FUTURE

There is no reason to believe that simply providing the schools with microcomputers will do much to improve education. Indeed, the thrust of our experience in the United States gives us every reason to believe that doing so will mostly be a waste. Time and time again we have flooded the schools with new instructional technologies . . . always to be disappointed in the end.
—Jim Rutherford, President,
American Association
for the Advancement of Science, 1984

When television spread like wildfire through the homes of Americans in the 1950s, there were numerous prophecies of its impact on education . . . a revolution in education was predicted with television as its foundation. What happened? Nothing like a revolution.
—Harold Howe II,
former U.S. Commissioner
of Education, 1983

The fourth myth I want to consider says that the lessons of the past about introducing new technology are clear and obvious. Learning from the past is much more difficult than is often assumed, and experts' recommendations don't completely deal with previous mistakes. Authorities have made four major recommendations based on prior experience with advanced technology. They suggest (1) developing plans to use computers, (2) establishing training programs, (3) funding programs to evaluate and develop better software, and (4) supporting research on the best way to use computers. If followed, however, these proposals will be great for university professors and their graduate students, but not so beneficial for the youth in our schools.

Planning, training, and research can be valuable, but the details are critical, and other actions must also be taken if money is to be spent wisely. Five areas need attention.

ENCOURAGE AND ASSIST CREATIVE TEACHERS

University-based research and central office-developed plans probably will not do much to increase opportunities for exceptional teachers. The California-based Rand Corporation recently examined schools that experts cited as making unusually effective use of computers. The researchers discovered what has come to be known as the "vanishing computer-using teacher phenomenon." Outstanding teachers are leaving the classroom to become district computer coordinators or software developers for companies (Shavelson et al, p. 29). The study confirms that the most effective use of computers will be made by creative, thoughtful, skilled people. As the Rand investigators concluded, "If teaching conditions are not improved for successful computer-using teachers, microcomputer-based instruction may not achieve its potential, and children will not benefit fully from the technology" (Shavelson et al, p. 30).

The fact is that many of our finest teachers are deeply frustrated by the bureaucracies in which they work. The following stories illustrate some of those frustrations. Attempts to make effective use of computers must deal with these problems.

In one school district, a teacher's work won awards from a national educational computing magazine and a company producing educational software. But her district refused to permit her to teach other faculty how to use the software she had prepared. She was not allowed to attend workshops when national authorities came to speak.

In another school district, English teachers eager to experiment with computers and word processing were told that the district would be using computers only for teaching programming until it had developed a plan. The district administrators assumed that the most appropriate use of their district's computers was to teach high school students to write programs in the BASIC language. For several years, no computer was available to English teachers.

In still another school district, the school board earmarked twenty thousand dollars for the purchase of computers. When educators asked how much was available to purchase software, they learned that the district's plan provided only five hundred dollars for the current school year. Teachers pointed out that that amount was not really enough to get the district started in a meaningful way. When they asked why they hadn't been consulted in the development of the plan, the teachers were told that school board and administration members thought the amount was sufficient. Teachers in one district reported that their superintendent told the school board, "We'll have to wait for the present generation of teachers to leave the schools before we can make effective use of computers. The older teachers are just too threatened by and uncomfortable with technology."

Teachers aren't the only ones who feel undermined by the educational system's response to computers. Parents—a free, experienced, available source of computer expertise—are often ignored by educators. In some communities, parents find school administrators and teachers prefer that parents confine their school involvement to planning bake sales. In these schools, parents are viewed as a threat, rather than a resource. Parents in one school asked if they could bring word-processing software from home to use with their children on the school's computer. The administrator refused permission, explaining that the school's computer was reserved for instruction in and practice with LOGO. At another school a parent whose job was to teach programming to engineers offered to teach a beginning programming course at his son's high school. He called the school's principal several times per week for five months before being allowed to work with a few students.

It's all too easy to find these examples of frustration in our schools. John Goodlad, former dean of the UCLA School of Education, studied one thousand classrooms all over the country. He concluded that teachers have many creative ideas that they are not allowed to use. The problems are not just financial; the system discourages creativity. As Goodlad reported, "The cards are stacked against deviation and innovation" (Goodlad, p. 15). In 1966 about fifty-three percent of public school teachers said they certainly would go into teaching if they could choose again. In 1981, however, the figure was twenty-two percent: only about one in five (Dearman and Plisko, p. 106).

But some schools have been able to move ahead rapidly to make sophisticated use of computer technology. What made the difference? What happened in schools where advanced applications of computers developed? Here are some answers.

- In Ortonville, Minnesota, the school superintendent encouraged individual teachers to find ways computers could extend and enrich learning. Teachers were not told what programs and applications they had to use. They were given freedom, encouragement, and the opportunity to learn. The school district recognized that it could gain by employing a person who was a computer whiz, despite his lack of teacher certification. Expectations that many teachers would use computers led to a situation where several of the most enthusiastic and effective programs were being supervised by teachers with twenty-five to forty years of experience. The school provided a variety of ways for students to learn about computers, rather than mandating a computer literacy class for each of its students. And one of the most successful and popular computer applications brought the school and community closer together, as students learned to help their parents run more cost-effective farms.
- At the East Consolidated Elementary School in St. Paul, Minnesota, the district administration gave the school principal and teachers considerable opportunity to develop their own program. The school's faculty agreed to take a few more students per class, permitting one teacher to spend full time in the school's computer lab supporting the other teachers. The district administration recognized that important and exciting things were happening in the lab and provided additional resources to the school so that experiments with word processing and LOGO could continue. The district also provided opportunities for the computer lab teacher to share some of what she had learned with other faculty.
- In Hartford, Connecticut, an outstanding teacher was given the opportunity to establish a special computer project with certain students. "Project Adventure" stimulated and challenged the brightest students. Youngsters reported that they liked being able to combine classroom and community experiences. They also

had fun thinking up ways to "spice up the program." Students did not use commercially prepared software to learn about their city—they created a package for others to use. Knowing that they were creating something that would help other students learn more about their community made the youngsters taking part feel worthwhile and important. The teacher involved acknowledges that he had to rethink the project several times and that others can learn from his mistakes.

- In the Oxford, Massachusetts, school district, administrators and teachers admitted that the schools were not succeeding with all the students. The district didn't increase graduation requirements, standardize courses, and announce it was committed to excellence. Instead, it recognized that everyone does not learn in the same way, at the same pace, in the same setting. The district didn't tell parents it was their fault the teenagers were in trouble. Rather than criticizing and punishing these youngsters, it developed a program that would help them succeed. Administrators and teachers were willing to let talented, caring Digital Equipment employees work directly with students. And the partnerships were viewed as mutually rewarding, rather than all one-way.

These positive programs provide a number of critical lessons that go beyond training and planning.

- There is no one best system to reach all the students.
- Teachers need opportunities to grow. The most effective programs are developed cooperatively, rather than imposed.
- Teachers appreciate opportunities to spend part of their day working with students, and part of the day with other kinds of responsibilities.
- There are important roles in educational computing for people who are knowledgeable but do not have formal teacher certification. School districts should have the flexibility to hire them and use their expertise.

- Schools do not have to wait for good software to be developed in order to make creative and effective use of computers. Some software was not originally developed for schools, but has been adapted to help stimulate and challenge young people.
- The most effective educators will continue to grow, develop, and refine their programs. They will respond to changes in hardware, software, and employment opportunities.
- Some of the most effective and popular programs involve combining classroom work with community service. This helps bring the school and community closer together and provides excellent motivation for students.
- Traditional male-female career goals remain strong. Any program planning to expand students' thinking must take explicit, continuing steps to encourage and assist nontraditional thinking.
- Many students say using a computer is fun. But using their creativity and stretching their imagination is probably more fun (and worthwhile) than simply having the computer make pleasant noises, compliment them for good work, or show them bright pictures.

No planning, training, or funding will lead to effective use of computers if creative teachers and knowledgeable community members are not permitted to provide leadership and create distinctive programs. It's true that some educators are selfish and shortsighted, and some parental volunteers make promises they don't keep. But to restrict all educators and community members because of a few failures will be to doom educational computing to a minimal role inside our schools. The first step to effectively using computers in schools is to change attitudes toward teaching and learning.

PROVIDE THE BEST POSSIBLE TRAINING

Most people know where roads paved with good intentions lead. The best plan in the world won't help students much if people don't have a good idea about how to carry it out. And right now there are critical problems in training people to make the most effective use of computers. The president of CBS Educational and Professional Publishing recently told a Congressional Subcommittee on Science, Research, and Technology,

> We have concluded that the lack of teacher training on micros is the biggest single impediment to their use. There is neither an existing structure nor one on the horizon to provide this training (Bonner, p. 71).

There are many ideas about how to provide this needed training, but some of them are not well thought out. A former U.S. Commissioner of Education wrote, "For those teachers already in the classroom, computer companies should provide short-term summer seminars and perhaps scholarships to keep them up to date on the use of technology as a teaching tool" (Boyer, 1984, p. 85). This is an attractive idea to some companies—and they are following up on it. IBM, Apple, and Radio Shack have provided funds to several school districts for training. Should anyone be surprised that IBM, Apple, and Radio Shack machines are being used in the training? Is what's good for IBM (or Apple or Commodore or Radio Shack) necessarily what's good for students? Will teachers hear about outstanding educational software if it's not available for use on the machines produced by the company sponsoring the training? Will educators get objective views about how to select machines when one company is sponsoring their training?

New York City public school teachers have had experience with courses taught by representatives of computer companies. According to Mike Ryan, director of the district's Computer and Information Science Unit, "Teachers who have taken courses taught by fellow teachers and corporate representatives say there is no comparison. A lot of times those corporate courses push their machine. Teachers resent that. They find the courses taught by fellow educators to be much more objective and useful in relating to the classroom situation." In this intensely competitive field, it's important to have training provided by the most objective and experienced people available. Those probably will not be staff hired by one computer company or another. While it's attractive to get teacher-training funds from companies producing machines, it's probably not the best way to proceed.

A second approach to teacher training is quite familiar: make teachers take university courses. Former U.S. Commissioner of Education Ernest Boyer strongly supports this notion. He recommends that "ten Technology Resource Centers be established on university campuses —one in each major region of the nation" (Boyer, 1983, p. 194). This is not a particularly good idea. Ask most educators what they think of the education departments at universities, and you're apt to get negative responses. There is not deep affection or respect among teachers for college professors (and that is a strong understatement). It's neither fair nor accurate to say that *all* university professors are out of date on the subject of computers and students. However, much of the most interesting, creative, and important development, thinking, and writing about learning and computers has been done by classroom teachers.

Teachers who've worked extensively with computers report they know much more than many university professors, who are supposed to be teaching teachers. A teacher from rural Indiana told colleagues at a recent national educational computing conference that she was there "because most Indiana colleges don't know anything about the educational use of computers except how to teach programming." A Nebraska school administrator reported that he had been able to find very little at universities that would help him develop effective educational computing programs in his school. Scott Evans, an Illinois elementary public school teacher who has helped set up a number of educational computing conferences, says that "university professors who come to our conferences have little to teach us. They come to learn from people who are doing it in the classroom."

It's sad to realize how often the views and expertise of classroom teachers are discounted or ignored. The National Science Foundation sponsored a three-day conference in December 1980 to discuss "National Goals for Computer Literacy in 1985." More than seventy people attended, including several *former* teachers. But only one was a classroom teacher at the time of the conference, according to the identification provided in the conference report (Seidel, Anderson, and Hunter, pp. 305-08). A major Minnesota conference center held a statewide meeting to discuss advanced technology and the schools. None of the major speakers were teachers, and only a few of the invited participants were teachers.

Leroy Finkel, an author and coordinator of educational computing for the San Mateo, California, public schools, agrees that we need to involve classroom teachers in leadership roles. "We've set up fifteen regional centers to help teachers learn to use computers in California schools. We just couldn't wait for the college professors to catch up. The real educational computing experts in California are the pioneering teachers."

The state of Minnesota has made a conscious decision to offer teachers the opportunity to learn about computers from other experienced teachers. Legislators provided funds for a decade to the Minnesota Educational Computing Corporation (MECC) so that the organization could run training programs for teachers around the state. Many of the MECC staff members are former teachers who can answer the detailed questions educators ask.

The city of New York has a cadre of outstanding classroom teachers who lead after-school workshops for other educators. The district has established one hundred satellite training centers around the city for the twenty-two separate courses it offers to educators. "Within a week of the time these courses are announced, they're full," explains Mike Ryan. "I'm sure these fine teachers don't do the after-school work for the money. It's plenty hard to work with kids all day, and then to spend two more hours with adults. And the pay isn't all that great—$600 a course for fifteen weeks, two hours per session. But the evaluations we get back are excellent." Teachers would rather take the district's courses than those at some local universities, and the district has developed a cooperative relationship with New York University and Long Island University. The two schools now accept the district's in-service computing courses for graduate credit. The outstanding classroom teachers who provide leadership have become adjunct university professors.

If real progress is to be made in competent training, there must be opportunities to learn from people who have been effective with real students in real schools. This means that opportunities should include those available in California, New York, or Minnesota. Training is provided by teacher centers, cooperative school district-university programs, and organizations staffed with former and part-time teachers with extensive, successful experience using computers with students.

CREATE SCHOOL-COMMUNITY PARTNERSHIPS

Computers have pulled the school and community more closely together in Blue Earth, Minnesota, a town of four thousand people about 150 miles south of a major metropolitan area.

In 1981, the district had funds to purchase computers and software, but lacked an informed catalyst who could help them move ahead. Ken Queensland had been the district's superintendent for more than twenty years. He knew the community, and he felt it would benefit from a strong program using computers throughout the schools. Gary Honken, Blue Earth's elementary school principal, felt the district's use of technology suffered from the lack of a coordinator. People didn't know where to turn for trustworthy software reviews, and it could take several days or even weeks to resolve problems with machines or software. Both Honken and Queensland agreed that the district needed a knowledgeable person who could react quickly to problems.

Darwin Oordt, a concerned parent, agreed to head a group that would try to raise money to fund a community computer coordinator for three years. He felt that any successful large-scale fund-raising drive would require that townspeople see direct, immediate benefits, so the group decided to offer an attractive package to local businesses. Each business that would contribute to the computer coordinator fund would get concrete returns on its investment:

- Five hundred dollars' worth of free advertising in the regional advertising publication that Oordt owned. This advertising would not be directed toward the company's product, but would also name the company as a supporter of the computer project.
- The opportunity to send four people to workshops the computer coordinator ran for businesses.
- The opportunity to call on the computer coordinator for technical advice. A business could get assistance on anything from how to go about purchasing a computer and setting it up to adapting and operating various business programs.

Darwin Oordt and Ken Queensland knew their town well. They approached twenty-one businesses and service groups, and twenty agreed to contribute. They took pledges of more than $62,000 to fund a school/community computer coordinator for three years. A year after the cooperative project started, all of the twenty contributors were still with the program and paying their pledges.

For a coordinator, Queensland wanted a person who knew a great deal about computers and could work well with educators and business people. He did not exclude certified teachers, but eventually decided to hire a person who was not a certified teacher. Townspeople agreed that he found a gem in Suzan Sollie.

Sollie had degrees in both mathematics and computer science and had worked at a private college as an administrative programmer analyst. Her varied background enabled her to be equally comfortable talking about business balance sheets and educational excellence. She is familiar with a variety of business software and can help adapt it to particular needs. She will answer a brief technical question for a company, or set up a workshop for a firm's employees. She also describes what's happening with computers in the schools, serving as a continuing source of information for people who otherwise have little direct contact with elementary and secondary education.

Her expertise and skill give her considerable credibility in the small town, where people decide quickly who is worthy of trust. Bruce Hanson, a loan and marketing officer for the First Bank—Blue Earth, attended several sessions Sollie conducted for townspeople. He says that "she did a nice job of helping us understand ways businesses and schools can use computers." The sessions combined some history of computers with the opportunity to try out several applications. The bank has used Sollie's software several times to help resolve problems.

Jim Smith is plant manager for Telex, which manufacturers magnetic tape recorders in Blue Earth. He has sent about fifteen people to workshops that Sollie has put on and agrees that she gives people "a good understanding" of the role and limitations of computers.

Steve Fernholz, a sixth-grade teacher and the president of the Blue Earth Education Association, agrees that having a computer coordinator has "worked out really well." He describes Sollie as "very knowledgeable and responsive." He admits that there were some questions initially about the computer coordinator's job description, but they have been resolved. He thinks that computers are going to be a bigger part of education than many of the other advanced technologies that appeared in the last fifteen years.

Sollie appears to have a positive, mutually respectful relationship with most of the Blue Earth teachers. The partnership works because everyone agrees they can assist each other. Sollie helps teachers evaluate, order, and adapt software, and provides in-service workshops. But she recognizes that teachers know their students better than she does. Teachers and administrators set the educational goals; Sollie helps them use technology to achieve them.

"There was some initial concern about my position," she says. "But I tried to be helpful. When teachers saw I could do something for them and really contribute to the life of the school, most of them accepted me well. I've made a real effort to work individually with teachers, and to get back to them quickly when they ask for help."

The Minnesota Department of Education has recognized Blue Earth as a "technology demonstration site," which means that the district is trying exemplary and pioneering approaches to the use of educational computing. Among Blue Earth's innovations are a fourth-grade class in which each of the twenty-six students works with her or his own computer; a comprehensive computerized community resource file, listing books, films, and people in the town with various kinds of information; and extensive experimentation with word processing at the elementary and secondary levels.

The cooperative program pioneeered by Blue Earth contains lessons for folks in many places. Small towns with limited technological expertise might adopt the program with few modifications. Larger towns and cities might make some changes. For example, a portion of a city might have its own computer coordinator. The possibilities are limited only by individual creativity.

Blue Earth educators and townspeople make several recommendations to towns interested in creating a similar partnership.

1. The coordinator should be someone who understands both business and educational computing. The person should be familiar with various business programs and applications, such as payroll, general ledger, word processing, inventory control, database management, and spreadsheets.

2. The coordinator need not know all the best educational programs in each academic area, but must know sources of software reviews and understand the characteristics of good programs.

3. The coordinator's job description should be clear. Certain misunderstandings and opposition can be avoided if this is done early.

4. Diplomacy and tact are essential for the coordinator.

5. It's useful for the business community to take the lead in soliciting funds. Business people are used to educators "asking for a handout." They may be more receptive to a fellow business person trying to establish a cooperative program.

6. Don't insist on the coordinator having any particular academic background or degrees. Superintendent Queensland believes, "You're looking for the right combination of knowledge and human relations. And people can develop these things in various ways."

7. Make sure you keep people informed about what's happening. People talk in small towns, and although they may not directly confront administrators with their concerns, they will have some. You can't wait to hear about problems. You must aggressively share information.

8. Teachers must be involved in developing any plan to use computers. They have to feel that their tasks will be made easier or their efforts enhanced.

9. Recognize that creating such a computer coordinator position will not be popular with everyone. Try to listen to people's concerns, but don't let objections destroy the program.

10. Keep the goals of cooperation clearly in mind. In Blue Earth, the goal was not to hire a computer coordinator. The goal was to increase staff and community interest in, and involvement with, computers. The coordinator was a means toward that end. As businessman Darwin Oordt explains, "You have to design a cooperative program that benefits everyone. Businesspeople like to do something good, and like to have other people tell him he's doing good."

A Rochester, Minnesota, program illustrates another form of community collaboration involving computers. The local school district and IBM jointly hire several teachers each year. The district and corporation each pay half of the teachers' salary during the school year. IBM hires the teachers during the summer. The teachers help train IBM engineers to give public presentations, work with entry-level employees, and complete other projects. The corporation and school district and teachers' organization agree that everyone participating sees the program as successful; everyone gains.

These programs are particularly noteworthy because they respond to the "vanishing computer-using teacher" phenomenon described earlier. Allowing teachers to spend part-time in the classroom and part-time working with industry can have two important benefits. It brings people into education who otherwise might not consider the field. It keeps outstanding teachers in education who might otherwise leave.

Creating new opportunities will not completely solve the problem of attracting and retaining bright, talented people in education. Part of the answer must be increasing teachers' salaries. One way to generate more money for salaries is to decrease other expenses in a school district.

Robbinsdale, Minnesota, illustrates another kind of partnership that does that. The school district there has created an alternative junior high program called "Technology Learning Campus" (or TLC). The program is located in a large community center, and shares space with programs for senior citizens, a nursery school, the city's park and recreation program, a ballet school, a dental clinic, and career counseling-job training programs for adults. This space-sharing enables the district to save money on the costs of heat, light, and security, allowing Robbinsdale to put more money into educational activities. Families in the district are permitted to choose between their neighborhood junior high school and the TLC. Started in 1984, TLC presently enrolls about three hundred students, grades six, seven, and eight. The TLC program uses a wide range of advanced technology, including robotics, teleconferences, computers, and TV production equipment, as well as traditional audiovisual equipment.

ACHIEVE EQUITY

According to Dr. Ronald E. Anderson of the University of Minnesota, "Today, modern 'haves' often get access to new technology long before the 'have-nots.' If a technological innovation is more than a convenience, i.e., a tool for effective functioning or survival, then it will drive a deeper wedge between the rich and poor." Most people agree that it's not fair for students from affluent families to have more opportunity to work with computers than students from poor families. And it's not right to use computers in the most sophisticated ways with upper-class children, while using them in the least challenging ways with children from low-income groups. But simple agreement with that theory offers little help in actually establishing a more just system. What can be done to correct the situation Anderson describes, in which technology may create a less just, less equitable society?

It is not easy even to get accurate information on how many schools have computers and what they are doing with them. In the January 1985 issue of the highly respected educational journal *Phi Delta Kappan*, you could read on page 240 that by April 1984 there were about 350,000 computers in U.S. schools. On page 303, however, in another article, it was reported that "schools house 630,000 microcomputers"—a figure almost twice as large as the first.

Part of the problem is that practices are changing so fast. The number of schools with computers, and the number of computers in schools, has increased dramatically in the last several years. A Denver-based research company reported that the number of computers in the country's fifty largest districts almost doubled in the 1983-84 school year. The number increased from 36,835 to 73,570 (Quality Education Data, p. 1).

Access to computers varies dramatically, depending on one's income. One national study found that when comparing the schools in the twelve thousand wealthiest communities with the twelve thousand poorest, the computer gap remained about the same between 1982 and 1984, a time of dramatic increase in overall number of schools with computers.

Year	% of poor schools having at least one computer	% of affluent schools having at least one computer
1982	9%	31%
1983	20%	68%
1984	48%	74%

Source: Quality Education Data, 1984.

The disparity between affluent and low-income families continues at home. A 1983 national study by Louis Harris found thirty percent of those with an income of $50,000 or more had home computers, whereas only four percent of those with incomes of $15,000 or less had them. Anderson found that in the Minneapolis-St. Paul area between 1982 and 1983, home computer ownership doubled for those with an annual household income of $25,000 or more. Ownership did not increase at all for those with an income below $15,000.

What solutions have been proposed to increase equity? Some legislators have recommended allowing corporations to donate computers to schools, and permitting them to deduct the full cost of the contributions from their income taxes. Several years ago, the California legislature permitted computer producing corporations to donate products and deduct the costs. The major participant was Apple Computer Company, which had lobbied for the program. Apple donated one computer, supplies, and training to each school in the state. This was a multi-million dollar donation, but it was like trying to empty the ocean with a paper cup. Apple's donation of a single computer to a school in a low-income area didn't reduce the inequity between that school and a suburban school fifteen miles away with the same number of students and twenty computers. Corporate donations, no matter how well intended, do not appear to be sufficient to deal with the problem.

Another suggestion has been to have a massive influx of state and federal funds for computer purchases in school districts that serve low-income families. Several states have started programs to permit use of federal "block grants" for computer purchases. Jim Lengel, director of secondary education in Vermont's department of education, explained, "We discovered that more than half of the block grant money was going to purchase computers. But the affluent districts still had more computers and much more expertise about how to use them."

A major, federally funded national computer purchase has other problems. Providing millions, even billions, of dollars to purchase computers right now could be a real waste of money. Computer prices are coming down rapidly, and more powerful, less expensive, easier-to-use machines are being produced every few months. Many school districts have not developed effective training programs for their staff members on the uses of computers and thus have a shortage of people who know how to make sophisticated use of the new technology. Another problem with purchasing thousands of computers is that many school districts have developed rigid procedures that make it difficult for creative teachers to use the machines. Purchasing more computers will not necessarily alter these patterns.

If millions or billions are not allocated to purchase computers to solve the problems of inequity, what actions should be taken? University of Minnesota professor Ronald Anderson says the action most needed right now is a "major investment in planning and research directed toward charting a course" (Anderson, 1984, p. 26). Most authorities agree that the urban school district farthest along in "charting a course" is located in Houston, Texas. This is due partly to the fact that Houston is "a large school district with a 'property rich' tax base, able to make the financial commitment to a comprehensive department of technology that other school districts cannot afford" (Chion-Kenney, p. 11). However, Houston also has shifted priorities and redirected funds. For example, the district cut driver education, deciding that learning about computers and other technology was more important. The district has also used a portion of its federal Title I money to develop special technology programs in schools with many children from low-income families.

The Houston public schools have probably created a more sophisticated and thoughtful package of steps than any other district toward increasing opportunity for low- and moderate-income youngsters and their families to use computers. These steps include

- training parents to help their children improve basic skills using a computer;
- sponsoring summer computer camps, with free tuition for students from low-income families;
- placement of computers so that each elementary school serving low-income students has at least thirty computers, and establishment of a technology matching fund process that allows schools to fund half the price of hardware and software and parents to donate a matching amount;
- production and broadcast over public television of a thirty-minute program to help parents understand how computers will affect their children's lives;
- sponsoring an annual technology fair;
- developing partnerships with businesses in which programmers, systems analysts, and hardware engineers teach students;
- providing $1,500 to $2,000 stipends for outstanding teachers who have completed a 296-hour training program in technology and are willing to work in low-income areas;
- creating pilot programs in low-income neighborhood schools designed to help low functioning students develop "higher order thinking skills";
- establishing technology magnet schools in low-income neighborhoods;
- producing a videotape and accompanying manual (in both English and Spanish) for parents about computers;
- training for administrators. All 245 Houston principals have attended workshops on the equity issue and have been "cautioned about scheduling practices that would limit access by certain groups";
- developing software that can be used to teach English as a second language; and
- developing a mobile classroom (called a "Techmobile") that may be checked out by a school

and that is equipped with lasers, robots, networks, plotters, synthesizer, and other equipment that the district could not afford to have in each school. (The Anoka-Hennepin school district in suburban Minneapolis has developed the same kind of mobile classroom. Randy Johnson, coordinator of the Anoka-Hennepin project, says, "The district is able to provide in-service throughout our area. Teachers will come out of their buildings and into the mobile lab before school, during preparation time, during lunch or after school. Most of the schools in the suburban Minneapolis district have their own computer labs. But the mobile lab gives teachers an opportunity to examine new software and get experience with 'state of the art' machines").

Houston is not the only place developing new approaches to exposing low-income children to computers. The New York City schools have used some of the same techniques Houston used to reach families that might otherwise not be able to afford home computers. The district permits parents to take workshops offered by its faculty if the parents agree to use the knowledge to help the district. The district also conducted a computer camp for students during the summer of 1984. Students were allowed to check out the computers and take them home for several weeks after the camp ended.

All of the strategies developed by these various districts seem preferable to immediately purchasing a computer for every student (which I had overenthusiastically recommended in an earlier book, *Free to Teach*).

The question of justice must be considered by school boards, legislators, and taxpayers. From a cold, economic viewpoint, it's unwise to widen the gap between affluent and low-income, between high- and low-skilled people. Ignoring low- and moderate-income students who can and do want to learn will increase unemployment, frustration, and a greater likelihood of crime.

School districts should not stop buying computers, and federal and state governments should continue to allocate money for their purchase. But the rush to buy must be tempered with realism. Legislators and school board members must try to create policies that encourage creative educators, interested parents, and resourceful community members to work together. Partnerships and structural changes in education will be required if students from low-income families are to gain all they can from computers.

PLANNING HOW TO USE COMPUTERS IN SCHOOLS

Technology revolutions have also failed to touch the schools largely because purchases frequently have preceded planning.

—Ernest Boyer,
former U.S. Commissioner
of Education, 1984

In a 1984 report the National School Boards Association found that eighty-six percent of the public school districts surveyed had no policies or guidelines about what they would do with the computers they were rushing to purchase. While recommending caution in interpreting the study results, the association says, "The findings do provide a general overview of what is happening in some of our nation's school districts" (NSBA, p. 1). The question is, is this wise? Is it acceptable? Don't effective organizations try to develop policies and guidelines first, then carry them out? Yes, they do! And any effective use of computers in our schools will come only from following carefully formulated, creative policies.

An example of such policymaking is the Technology and Educational Improvement Act adopted in 1982 by the Minnesota legislature. One national school expert calls the Minnesota program "a model piece of legislation—one of the best I've seen" (*Electronic Learning*, Nov.-Dec., 1983, p. 42). Though it's not perfect, the Minnesota plan provides some guidance in thinking about how a district or state ought to plan for the use of computers and other advanced technology in its schools.

Specifically, the act encourages each of Minnesota's school districts to develop a written "technology utilization plan." This plan *must* be written in conjunction with a local advisory committee composed of parents, community members, and faculty. Each school district can apply for financial aid to develop the plan. The technology plan for each district must meet several criteria that are intended to encourage cooperation and community involvement. The plan must show

- how the district determined its needs and what it found;
- how the district will use technology to provide educational opportunities for people of all ages, including women, minorities, and the disabled residing in the district;
- what the district's goals are for implementing technology in management and instruction;
- how the district intends to meet those goals;
- how technology will be integrated into the district's community education program;
- how the district will evaluate its efforts in technology;
- how it will report results to the community;
- how the plan was developed in consultation with a state-mandated, local curriculum-advisory committee; and
- how the plan will be reviewed each year and how needed revisions will be made.

Each district must submit its plan to the Minnesota Department of Education for approval. Then the fun begins. Enough money has been allocated so that every district with an approved plan will receive $1.00 per student for staff training and another $1.60 per student to be applied toward the purchase of software on the education department's list of "high-quality software." The district may use state funds to pay no more than fifty percent of the cost of software on this list.

Before being listed, software is reviewed by five people. Three are classroom teachers, one is an expert on computers, and the last is the state education department's specialist on the curriculum area the software deals with (e.g., English, science, mathematics). Rankings are given in three areas: instructional characteristics, content characteristics, and technical characteristics. Software must receive at least seventy percent of the total possible points from the five reviewers in order to be placed on the approved list. As of early 1985, the education department had prepared three lists of high-quality software.

The process of submitting software to the education department for review is simple. A diskette and any accompanying material are simply sent to Dr. Gilbert Valdez at the Minnesota Department of Education in St. Paul. Valdez is manager of the section responsible for integrating technology into the curriculum of the state's schools.

The state's list will benefit school districts. In many instances, school districts have found it difficult to obtain review copies of new software products or to develop expertise in evaluating software. The state's list can seve as a buying guide for such districts. The plan is to update the list every six months.

Although districts may purchase software not included on the list, they will have to find other funds to pay for such products. Under this act, state funds can be used only for software on the department's approved list.

Another portion of the bill provided about $1.25 million to be shared by eight to ten model districts around the state. Those chosen sites received money to develop the most advanced, most exciting programs imaginable. About $300,000 has been allocated to allow other educators to visit these sites.

A key part of Minnesota's plan provides funds for training teachers. (The actual act was developed with a great deal of participation from Minnesota educators.)

The Minnesota Educational Computing Corporation (MECC) received money to work with school districts around the state. Some of MECC's staff are former teachers, and others on the staff have been working closely with teachers for more than a decade. Valdez notes that "the legislature recognized that training would have to be provided by people familiar with the practical as well as the theoretical aspects of using computers in schools."

Both state and local school officials say that the most effective training for teachers was conducted by people who are or have been teachers. Their experience gives the trainers credibility with other teachers and enables them to answer specific questions and provide creditable advice about implementing the plan.

Observers of the Minnesota plan hope that schools will be open to extremely creative and unusual applications of advanced technology. The act places extraordinary opportunities and responsibilities in the hands of local districts.

Overall, both the education department and local school officials are pleased with the law. Elmer Koch, a curriculum generalist for the Minneapolis public schools, says he's "very optimistic about the law's potential." Charles Lund, assistant director of math, science, and technology for the St. Paul public schools, agrees, calling it "a great opportunity to develop strong, effective programs."

However, Minnesota's plan did run into several problems during its first year of implementation. Since learning from other people's mistakes is as valuable as learning from their successes, let's look briefly at a couple of the problems.

The first major one concerned politics, that constant companion of reform. Fifty proposals were submitted to the Department of Education in response to its request for eight to ten exemplary technology demonstration sites. The department carefully reviewed proposals, using a statewide task force of educators. They ranked the proposals and then made recommendations to the State Board of Education, which made the final selection.

The state board's decisions immediately created both "sound and fury." Instead of funding the three most highly rated proposals, the board picked proposals from congressional districts in which its members lived. One of the funded projects was ranked thirty-third, another fortieth. Two different evaluation systems apparently were being used: the state department ranked on the basis of quality, the board selected on the basis of geographic distribution. Some board members felt that several of the highly rated districts already had an advantage: they were suburban communities with considerable sophistication about computers and other advanced technology. These board members wanted to spread the state's dollars around more extensively than funding the highest-ranking proposals would permit.

The board of education came under a great deal of criticism. Deciding that the board's decisions couldn't be reversed, the legislature allocated funds for another group of exemplary projects, including the four most highly ranked projects that had not been funded.

A second problem was the list of state-approved software. Some people felt it was inappropriate for the State Department to act as a "censor" for local districts, telling them what they could purchase with state funds. And the daily introduction of new software created an ongoing dispute for state-approved lists. Teachers have expressed frustration with the state's slow process of reviewing software. For example, outstanding software for problem-solving had been identified and submitted to the state. However, six months later, the software still had not been reviewed.

(Interestingly enough, after considering the possibility of a similar kind of state-approved software list, California decided not to establish one. Leroy Finkel, Instructional Computing Coordinator for the San Mateo Office of Education and author of fourteen books about computing, had several objections to such lists. "They are always out of date and they are too limiting," he says. Instead, he urges states to create criteria by which educators can judge software.)

A third problem with Minnesota's plan concerned a fundamental problem in public education: the difficulty of getting educators to learn from each other! Recently the state education department sponsored a two-day workshop in the Minneapolis-St. Paul area that featured each of the exemplary technology demonstration projects and provided teachers with an opportunity to learn from people from throughout the state. Yet despite extensive publicity, many of the area districts, including some of the state's largest, did not send any representatives.

Ed Mako, a teacher from Lakeville, Minnesota, who is pioneering the use of word processing in high schools, offers another example. An article about Mako's work and research appeared in the Minnesota Department of Education's monthly newspaper, more than 50,000 copies of which are distributed to educators throughout the state. But only eight individuals and two of the state's 435 school districts asked him for more information. And not a single university professor wrote. Not one.

Even though there are problems with Minnesota's plan, at least that state *has* a plan—a concrete policy to follow to implement the use of computers in its school districts. Every other state needs one, too. As someone once said, "When you don't know where you are going, any path will take you there."

There are a number of characteristics common to the successful plans I've examined. Successful plans
- provide training by highly qualified, skillful instructors. The instructors must know a good deal about the day-to-day challenges educators face;
- increase parental and community knowledge about the appropriate use of computers. These should include programs at schools and, if at all possible,

opportunities to use computers in homes and community centers;

- assist and encourage female, handicapped, and minority youngsters to use computers;
- are flexible enough to make revisions as new technological and software breakthroughs appear;
- define the criteria that educators should use to evaluate software (see also Chapter 11);
- provide opportunities for outstanding educators to spend part of their time working with students, part of it training others, and part of it working with universities and corporations to develop new technologies and applications;
- provide additional pay for outstanding educators who work a longer school day or longer school year, or have additional responsibilities because of their expertise;
- fund research *only* if it involves partnerships between schools and universities and/or corporations;
- recognize the need for nontraditional models for youth. It's important for both young men and young women to see women and people of color teaching courses in which computers are used;
- create opportunities for young people to visit and learn from organizations where various advanced technologies are being used. Internships and apprenticeships should be widely available;
- recognize the significant differences between metropolitan and "outstate" schools, with special consideration given to adapting programs and projects to meet needs and build on strengths of rural areas;
- use mobile classrooms with advanced technology to work with communities and educators in remote parts of a state;
- review school policies and procedures in light of the availability of home computers; and
- provide cooperative training programs involving outstanding classroom teachers and universities.

We must go beyond the kinds of recommendations made by the President of the American Association for the Advancement of Science, who testified at a Congressional hearing on June 5, 1984, and called for the creation of a Council for the Use of Computers in Education to oversee planning and to advise Congress and the appropriate federal and state agencies. He also urged that the federal government fund an independent corporation to design, build, and maintain a modern educational telecommunications system linking schools and colleges with sources of creative audiovisual learning materials. He said there are many creative people who can produce good instructional materials: "They are located in universities, museums, public television stations, government agencies, and in profit-making and nonprofit organizations" (Rutherford, p. 6).

But aren't there any capable people in schools? When does the voice of the creative teacher get heard? Where is the insistence that research projects be operated cooperatively between school districts and universities? Where is the demand that teachers have opportunities to learn from fellow teachers, rather than spend more time in outdated, irrelevant university courses?

The real lessons of the past *are not* simply that planning and training must proceed the introduction of technology. Plans can be liberating or limiting. Training can be challenging or choking. The demands for planning and training often assume that national commissions, university professors, and central office administrators have some greater wisdom—some keener insight into truth. It just isn't so.

The most important lesson from the past is that the people working directly with kids must have opportunities to experiment, create, and share with others. Not all of their ideas will be good—the best teachers eagerly acknowledge that they have much to learn. But progress requires partnerships. It can't be the anointed telling the dummies how to do it. Partnerships require mutual respect, and the sharing of opportunities and resources.

**MYTH 6: All responsible parents who
can possibly afford it should buy
computers for their children.**

8

PARENTS AND COMPUTERS

It's never too early to begin.

—National Magazine Ad
for Software, 1984

This chapter analyzes the most personal myth: all
responsible parents who can possibly afford it should
buy computers for their children. For must of us,
accepting or rejecting this myth will have the most
direct effect on our families and our checkbooks.

Many parents have become convinced that, in the
words of one advertisement, "it's never to early to
begin" working with computers. Thousands of parents
have already purchased computers so their children
won't be left behind. After all, ads tell us that by buying
a computer we're helping our children do better in
school, get into better colleges, and be better prepared
for the twenty-first-century job market. Of course, parents want those advantages for their children, but
before we buy the claims *and* the computers, we need to
apply some criteria regarding computer purchases for
our children.

Any parent considering the purchase of a home computer must remember that the technology is changing
dramatically and rapidly. Less than two years after its

purchase, the computer on which this book was written (an Apple III) was widely available at *half* its original cost, with *twice* the original power. (And recently the company announced that it will no longer produce this model.) Prices will continue to drop for most computers, and many new products will have features that older ones did not. An Apple Computer Company publication accepts this, noting, "For years to come, computers that do more for less will continually appear" (Lundstrom, p. 39). Nevertheless, computer companies and enthusiasts ask people, "Will the disadvantages of one's current computerlessness be outweighed by the advantage of a future price reduction?" (Lundstrom, p. 39). Corporations and computer magazines tell parents that their children cannot afford to wait—they need the benefits of a computer *now*.

But a primary consideration ought to be the age of the child. Not all age groups of children unquestionably gain from the use of computers. Anyone contemplating a computer purchase primarily for children ought to look first at just what the computer can help a child of a specific age accomplish.

SHOULD YOU BUY A COMPUTER FOR CHILDREN UNDER AGE FIVE?

I don't think so. If your children are under age five, consider waiting a few years. As of early 1985, virtually all the software available for children of this age group does things with and for children that parents can do much less expensively themselves.

Much of the software aimed at this very young age group is a variation on the matching-identification theme. With it, the computer functions as a drill-and-practice machine. The screen shows a letter or number and asks the child to press the matching button on the keyboard. If the child is successful, a face smiles, or fireworks go off, or something else designed to be pleasant happens.

Here are some examples. One such piece of software, called Getting Ready to Read and Add (by Sunburst), was designed by a parent. A bird opens its mouth and numbers, letters, or shapes come out. When the child answers correctly, a small bird flies up toward the top of the screen. When an incorrect answer is given, the computer makes a brief noise. The software can be customized by controlling the selection of numbers and letters. Sunburst says the series of programs is "designed to teach shape discrimination and letter and number recognition." The graphics are unquestionably good.

Another well-known product of this type is Early Games for Young Children by Springboard Software. The author is a former public school teacher who designed the software for his own children. There are six programs on the disk. Several are of the letter and number identification variety. The same principle is used, with positive rewards given for a correct answer and a brief noise for inaccurate responses. Early Games has two other noteworthy programs. One asks that a word be typed into the computer (which a parent or older child can do). Then the younger child is asked to type in the word. If the child does it successfully, the word is flashed across the screen several times in ever larger and more dramatic fashion. (Our children used this happily, learning to type their names at age three.) Another program allows a child to draw pictures on the screen using a dot that can be moved in any direction, creating various lines, shapes, and patterns. The child can also change the color of the dot by pushing the space bar.

There are dozens of other programs of this sort published for the preschool market by various companies. But parents must ask themselves if it's worth buying a $500 to $2,000 computer for their small children to do these kinds of things, when they can do them without computers. It's easy to cut out different shapes, numbers, or letters from construction paper, or buy them ready-made for a nominal price. Parents, grandparents, and older brothers and sisters can all take turns playing learning games with young children. There are a number of good books that parents can buy or check out of the library to help children gain this same knowledge and learn these same skills. And of course *Sesame Street*, from the Children's Television Workshop, helps millions of young children learn letters, numbers, and shapes. Young children need time with their parents. They need parental encouragement. Fancy graphics and positive reinforcement from a machine are *not* adequate substitutes for direct contact with parents.

Many parents are extremely busy and find it difficult to spend time with their young children. But if time is the problem, it would be much better for the parent to spend the money these disks cost to hire someone to do housework or whatever, and spend the resulting free time doing these activities with the child. If money is not an issue, than it will be better spent on books that a parent reads to his or her children. There is an enormous amount of research showing that one of the best ways to prepare children to enjoy reading, and do it well, is to read to them from infancy.

For families that can't afford computers or books, the library is an important resource. And it becomes critical for social service agencies working with low-income parents to help them learn how to teach their children prereading skills.

There are a few other software packages available for the young that may make a parent's decision about purchasing a computer more complicated. One, produced by Springboard Software, is called Mask Parade. The disk contains six programs that enable children to design their own masks, jewelry, badges, hats, and glasses. Children select from about a dozen faces, eyes, noses, and mouths (or they can draw their own) and then print out what they construct. One valuable dimension of Mask Parade is that it's simple enough that one youngster can show another how to use it, and even four- to five-year-olds can get good at it. But it also is complex enough to give the person who understands it the feeling that she or he has mastered something meaningful.

This program does encourage some other healthy tendencies: creativity, and a view of the computer as a powerful machine that can be used to help solve problems or create useful products. On the other hand, parents can work with their young children to help them design masks. You can purchase books that provide masks that children can color. Children can also design masks using paper bags and pictures from magazines. You don't need a computer, and the computer really can't do it much better.

Other disks available for young children help them learn a computer's keyboard. The Friendly Computer by MECC has matching and action game programs that help users learn where certain keys are. Another program on the disk helps children learn various computer terms (diskette, monitor, disk drive, keyboard, and computer). And the disk also includes a program that allows youngsters to draw pictures and increase their skills in logic and planning.

Still other programs exist to help preschoolers learn basic mathematics functions. For example, Computer Math Activities, by Addison-Wesley, features a number of games that reward players who can add, subtract, multiply, or divide numbers quickly. The rewards come in several forms. In one game, children who supply correct answers see a basketball player shoot a ball through the hoop (an incorrect question brings a missed shot). Another game allows participants to cover up any of several different dinosaurs (this was extremely popular with the four-year-olds who tried it). The quicker they answer a math problem correctly, the faster the dinosaur is covered. Another game on the disk allows the person answering questions correctly to shoot at stars (rather than at people, which I object to). Fast, correct answers bring more shots. Another important feature of the program is that its complexity can be adjusted, depending on the age or skill of the child using it. It can be as simple as adding 1 and 1 or as complex as multiplying 9999 by 9999.

These programs sound attractive, and children ages three and up have played and enjoyed all these games. But by themselves do they justify the purchase of a computer primarily intended for use by a preschooler? In the end, of course, each family has to arrive at its own answer. But my answer remains no. Parents can find a variety of noncomputer games that cost much less but teach their children the same skills. Many inexpensive mechanical devices test math skills and provide a positive response for correct answers. You don't need an expensive computer to drill children in arithmetic.

When my wife was pregnant in 1978 with our twins, we looked at home computers. We talked with a number of salespeople, and most of them encouraged us to wait a few years before buying a computer for our children. They explained that there weren't enough programs available for infants to justify purchasing a computer primarily intended for their use. They gave us good advice, though they lost a sale. In the years since our children were born, the basic computer we looked at shortly before they arrived has become four times more powerful while costing less than half of what it did then. And in the last couple of years, many new computer applications have developed that didn't exist before. All the experts expect the same kind of thing to happen in the next five years.

In summary, the software available in early 1985 for use with children under age five convinces me that it's worth waiting a few years before buying a computer primarily intended for their use. But there is one exception to this guideline. Some handicapped or disabled children ages three to five have been able to make remarkable progress with computer assistance, even though traditional methods of learning and communication had not worked for them. If you are convinced that a computer can help your child as nothing else has, it's not too soon to make the purchase. But it will be vital to inform yourself about equipment, software, and training. This field is new, and many professionals have limited knowledge.

SHOULD YOU BUY A COMPUTER FOR CHILDREN AGES FIVE TO TEN?

Maybe, maybe not. This is a more difficult question than the previous one. The following quiz is not intended to provide a precise, scientific answer to this question, but it may help you make up your mind. You may decide to give different value to the various questions, and you may want to include other questions. All the issues listed, however, should be considered before you buy a computer for your school-age children.

Take this test yourself and, when appropriate, give it to your children, adding up the points indicated for each yes answer. For every question but the last one, a negative answer counts as zero. When the word *child* is used, it means one or more people in your family ages five to ten.

If your child's elementary school has computers, please answer these questions:

1. Does your child's teacher tell you that he or she displays a great deal of interest in using the school's computer? *(2 points)*
2. Does your child's teacher tell you that he or she displays considerable or unusual skill in using the school's computer? *(7 points)*

Regardless of whether your child's school has computers, please answer these questions:

3. Does your child seem to be extremely interested in writing? *(1 point)*
4. Does your child have difficulty writing? *(1 point)*
5. Does your child say that he or she is not challenged by school, that the work is too easy? *(1 point)*
6. Do you have enough money to buy a printer and a monitor for any computer you buy? *(2 points)*

7. Do you have at least several hundred dollars that can be used to purchase software for a computer during the first year you own it? *(2 points)*

8. Do you have an older child who is knowledgeable about computers and willing to help you and your younger child learn how to use computers? *(2 points)*

9. Are you concerned about how much television your child watches? *(1 point)*

10. Are there programs available in your community to help parents learn how to use computers in appropriate ways with their children? *(3 points)*

11. Is there a place within a reasonable distance of your home where you can have a computer repaired? *(2 points)*

12. Is there someone in your home who is capable of repairing a computer if it has problems? *(4 points)*

13. Is there a group of people in your community who own the kind of computer you are considering purchasing and have formed a "user group"? *(1 point)*

14. If the answer to the preceding question is yes, would you consider going to meetings to learn more about using your home computer? *(2 points)*

15. Do you have some familiarity with computers because of your work? *(3 points)*

16. Do you feel any personal curiosity or interest, not motivated by fear or guilt, about getting a computer for your home? *(2 points)*

17. Does your child have a handicap or disability that makes it difficult for her or him to learn in a traditional manner? *(7 points)*

18. Do you have a friend who is knowledgeable about computers and would be willing to help you think about your decision and share her or his experiences? *(2 points)*

19. Do you have a friend who is knowlegeable about computers and who would be willing to help you examine the various computers that are available and go with you to various stores to look at them? *(3 points)*

20. Are you willing to spend several hours per week for two to three months to help your child learn various

ways to use a computer in your home? *(10 points for a yes, but subtract 10 if the answer is no)*

Before you figure out your score, you may want to look over this brief discussion of the questions and rationales for the points I've suggested.

1. A child who is already interested is much more likely to enjoy, and gain from, using a computer. In this, it's like any other major gift. Think about the presents you bought your children that you thought they'd like, but that they ended up not doing much with. You probably don't want to spend the money and time on a computer unless your child shows significant interest.

2. The combination of interest and skill is a real winner.

3. One of the major educational applications of computers is word processing. Word processing makes it much easier for people to edit their writing. Eager writers sometimes blossom with computers because they can spend so much more time on the creative parts, and so much less time on the drudgery.

4. Research shows that youngsters who have not enjoyed writing very much sometimes become enthusiastic when they have the opportunity to learn word processing.

5. You have a good deal to think about if you're getting this message from your child. And despite the commercials, don't think that computers are necessarily the answer. In an earlier book, *Free to Teach*, I described ways that schools and parents could work together to make learning more challenging and rewarding—and most of the ideas do not require spending more money, much less buying a computer for your home. However, computers can help provide some challenge and stimulation for youngsters.

6. Some of the most important educational uses of computers require the ability to print out what has been written or produced. Not having a printer means cutting out a major computer application (word processing). The monitor is extremely desirable. Despite what the advertisements say, it's not

enough to have a color television set to hook your computer up to if you want to use word processing or other applications that require reading words on the screen. Most televisions are not set up to produce clear text from a computer.

7. Many of the most valuable educational uses of computers require software. Each disk will cost a minimum of $15. Most of the best will cost at least $30, and many will be $40-60.

8. Such a person can save you many frustrating hours. Moreover, the interaction can be a great way to bring a family together and to build up the self confidence of the knowledgeable child.

9. Did this question surprise you? In fact, some parents are reporting that after they purchase a computer for their children, the television is silent much more often.

10. You'll be a long way ahead if you take some kind of class about home computing. It's best if such a course is in your child's school (since you'll learn how the computer is used there, and can coordinate your use), but a good course not associated with the school is still better than no course at all.

11. Like other electrical appliances, computers sometimes break or get tired. You'll need access to some place that can fix yours when this happens.

12. If the answer to this question was yes, you are extremely lucky. Computers, like televisions, can be expensive to repair.

13. "User groups" have saved many people from total confusion and exasperation with their computers. Frequently, people in these groups know much more about a particular computer than the salespeople do. Sometimes, they know things even the manufacturer doesn't.

14. It doesn't help much to have a nearby user group if you wouldn't be willing to participate.

15. Using computers at work will give you a real head start. Though your children won't be using computers as you do, you already know some computer terms and probably have a general sense of some computer capabilities.

16. Kids learn a great deal from watching the adults around them (it's how they learn to walk and talk, for example). If you are genuinely interested in fishing, going to a museum, taking a hike, going camping, etc., your young child probably will be much more likely to share that interest. Virtually all children ages five to eight will need a great deal of help in working with a computer from an adult with whom they feel comfortable.

17. As earlier chapters documented, many parents of handicapped/disabled youngsters are finding that computers help their children achieve in ways previously not thought possible.

18. A knowledgeable friend can save you many hours and thousands of dollars. The world of computers has its own jargon. You'll want to know about the experiences of people you know and trust, not just those of a writer, like me, whose experience and values may be very different from yours.

19. Salespeople are not there to protect you, but to sell. A friend can help you cut through the "computer-speak" and make an informed, reasonable decision.

20. This is a critical question. Your child will probably need help from you in using the computer. If you can't spend time helping, strongly consider waiting to buy a computer until you are not as busy.

Now calculate your score. A total of 60 points is possible.

45-60 points. What are you waiting for? It's surprising that you haven't already bought a computer.

30-45 points. Strongly consider purchasing a computer to use with your child.

20-30 points. Do some additional reading. Your child may benefit from a computer, but it's far from certain.

Fewer than 20 points. It's unlikely, unless your child is a genius who can move ahead with very little support or assistance, that buying a computer for your home right now is a good idea.

SHOULD YOU BUY A COMPUTER
FOR CHILDREN AGES ELEVEN TO EIGHTEEN?

As children get older, the question becomes more difficult to answer. Teenagers are able to do a lot more for themselves. There are several well-developed programs available today that make excellent use of computer capabilities and can probably help your children in school. The two most well-known uses of computers for students of this age are word processing and programming.

As earlier chapters showed, students who use a computer's word-processing capability tend to spend more time revising and polishing their writing. Word-processing programs will *not* teach your children to capitalize, punctuate, spell, or use grammar correctly. The power of these programs is in their ability to help people make corrections quickly and easily.

Children will make much better use of word-processing programs if they know how to type. In the future, typing may be much less important than it is today. Computers may be developed that rely primarily on people talking rather than typing into them. However, in the next five years, typing will continue to be valuable.

Fortunately, some excellent programs are available that can help youngsters learn to type. These programs are controversial, however, because some business education teachers think it a bad idea to use a typing program without the supervision of a person who has been trained to teach this skill. A later chapter on software explores this issue in more detail. But any parent who is purchasing a computer to help her or his children improve their writing ought to insist that they learn to type first.

Programming is the second major educational use of home computers. Many parents report that their children are asking for a computer so that they can learn or improve their programming skills. Like music, sports, dance, painting, or writing, programming can become a lifelong hobby or vocation.

Some young people, in fact, become master programmers by the time they are sixteen or seventeen. Many teenagers have written commercially successful software. In the Minneapolis-St. Paul area, for example, Eric Thorsell and Todd Murray established a company called Software Images. One of their programs, Typing Factory, helps youngsters improve their typing speed. It's every bit as good as, if not better than, many programs two or three times as expensive. Also, in the past few years, the Minnesota Educational Computing Corporation has hired more than a dozen high school students to help write software. The list of examples could go on and on.

So the purchase of a computer for a teenager might be viewed in the same light as purchasing a fine musical instrument. The same guidelines ought to apply:

1. A youngster should have demonstrated considerable interest in the subject before an expensive instrument or computer is bought.
2. The youngster should have opportunities to learn more about the instrument or computer at school, from a skilled professional, or from other talented, interested people.
3. Parents should feel comfortable with the youngster's interest. Parents who hate music will be annoyed by their child's practicing. Parents who fear or dislike computers won't like their teenager spending hours with a computer.

THE IMPACT OF COMPUTERS ON FAMILIES

If you decide to buy a computer for your child—not because you feel you have to, but because your child's age, capabilities, and interests indicate that it would be a wise decision—you need to be aware that the computer may have a significant impact on your family.

A study directed by Joseph B. Giacquinta, a professor of educational sociology at New York University, examined relationships in twenty families that had each acquired a computer for use in the home. The families lived in urban, suburban, and rural settings in New York, New Jersey, and Connecticut. The major findings of his study are as follows:

1. Computers did not change the underlying social organization of the families. If anything, computers "actually served to reinforce existing family patterns," according to Giacquinta (Collins, p. 1F).
2. Parents feared children would become overly involved with computers and pull away from friends and family. This generally did not happen.
3. In general, the computers were underused, and there was relatively little use made of professional educational software. Children used home computers primarily to play games.
4. The study identified four kinds of parents: those who "stood over" their children and gave directions; those who "stood by" their children in case they needed assistance or directions; those who "stood by wringing their hands," hoping that things would work out; and those who "stood aside," allowing their children maximum opportunity to decide how the computer should be used.

Conversations with families in a dozen states indicate that these four classifications are widespread. But wise parents will not settle for standing aside or handwringing. The most thoughtful parents play several roles in helping their children develop attitudes and knowledge about various subjects, and it should be the same with computers.

The first role is *modeling*. Children pick up a great deal by watching and listening to their parents. Parents should learn along with their children about computers. Mothers and fathers should show they are willing and eager to learn about computers. This will help convince children that learning really should be a life-long activity, not just something confined to school hours. Parents may wish to share information with schools, to borrow or loan programs, or to let social service agencies, community groups, or political groups use their computer. Parents who are unable to do other kinds of volunteer work may be able to help individuals or organizations by running off letters for the group, or by giving presentations about possible uses of the machine. All these actions will help young people develop positive values and constructive attitudes.

The second important role is *guidance*. Parents should discuss ethical questions about computer use and impact. They should encourage sharing and prohibit theft—the copying of other people's programs. Copying is a pervasive problem with computer programs. The technology makes it relatively easy to obtain other people's software without paying for it, and people who would not consider photocopying a friend's book are doing exactly that with computer programs. Parents also should encourage all members of the family to learn about computers, not just the one or two young-sters who are excited initially.

The third vital role is *assistance*. Children naturally look to their parents for help. Regardless of how much a youngster knows about computers, and how little a parent understands, there are ways the adult can help. Parents can encourage comparison shopping for software. They can subscribe to computing magazines. They can go to libraries, user-group meetings, and shows to learn together. Parents also can look for new ways to use computers. The New York University research showed that a number of families did not use word processing because they had never heard of it. The children's schools taught programming but did not use computers to help teach writing.

The wisest parents will view computers as they view other powerful, complex machines. Their children will learn how to understand and use them to help accomplish personal goals, to help other people, to solve problems. Young people will learn that in sharing and assisting others, we all gain.

MYTH 7: There is not much software
that can be used effectively to increase
learning.

9

USING COMPUTERS
TO SERVE OTHERS
AND SOLVE PROBLEMS

Teachers say the biggest problem is the dearth of quality
software—the computer instructions that make up the
teaching materials.
—Edward Fiske, *New York Times*, 1984

Some authorities insist that there is not much good educational software available. Many of the most thoughtful computer-using teachers and parents recognize that
this is a myth. They know that software not specifically
created for "education" can be extremely valuable.
These people have departed from the conventional path
and are creating outstanding learning opportunities for
children.

The next two chapters (9 and 10) describe a number of
creative, effective ways to increase learning by using
computers. (Chapter 11 offers some guidelines for buying educational software.) Teachers who are responsible
for the projects described here are not waiting for or
relying on software to cover concepts in the classroom
and they don't see the computer by itself as a revolu-
tionary instrument. They *do* think that combined with

other activities, the computer can help solve various problems. Some of the most sophisticated educational programs involve students using computers to help other people. The following projects illustrate how computers and creative educators can increase student motivation and skill.

CREATING CHANGES IN THE COMMUNITY

Since 1977, Folsom, Pennsylvania, high school students have been using their school's computers to help complete energy audits for townspeople. The program's coordinator, Nick Ignatuk, believes that "one of the most exciting ways of helping students to see the relevance of topics studied in the science classroom is by means of hands on experience in practical applications. He also notes that this is an excellent example of cooperation between a corporation and a school district. The Sun Oil Company helped the educators purchase equipment used in the energy audits.

The Pennsylvania students are trained in a physics class to recognize and investigate various weatherization and insulation techniques in a typical home. According to Ignatuk, students learn to determine building dimensions, window and door sizes, thermostat settings, construction materials, fuel types and costs, and insulation types and amounts. The data they gather about a particular building is then fed into a computer. The computer's program describes steps the family can take to make their home energy efficient, and then provides a list of local insulation and weatherization suppliers.

Evaluations of this program have been extremely positive. Students show an increased interest in class, and their grades have improved. The community likes the project. Everyone wins!

Across the country, another school has students making even more extensive use of computers to help their community. Students in Ortonville, Minnesota, are helping their families decide how to run their farms by analyzing options on the school's computers.

"When I first heard about computers," says Don Nolting, who has been raising sheep, hogs, and cattle in western Minnesota for more than thirty years, "I figured they were for businesses, not for farming. Then my daughter Angie brought home a printout she'd run at school. You could tell whether our farm was making or losing money by just looking at one sheet of paper, rather than going through a whole box of records. I'm really proud of what she's doing."

Sixteen-year-old Angie Nolting is just one of many students who are immersed in Ortonville's computer program. With leadership from Superintendent Burton Nypen, the local schools have one of the nation's most comprehensive, sophisticated computer programs. From kindergarten through twelfth grade, computers are incorporated into classes. Spreadsheet analysis, word processing, programming, simulations, drill-and-practice, computer-assisted instruction—it's all happening in Ortonville, a rural community of 2,200 people, located 175 miles west of Minneapolis-St. Paul. The townspeople strongly approve of Superintendent Nypen's attitude that computers should be viewed as tools, and the school continually thinks about ways to serve its community.

Ortonville's agricultural education instructor, Phillip Iverson, decided to explore computer applications in farming. (He helps his students learn to use VisiCalc and an agricultural template called F.A.R.M.—Farm Accounting and Records Management.) "It's obvious that farms are operating on smaller and smaller margins," he explains. "Only the most efficient farms are going to survive."

In more than twenty-five years of teaching, Iverson discovered that farm bookkeeping was often neglected. "You can only teach so much record keeping and then you lose a person's attention. It's so time consuming that it's often left in the lurch. But computers are very appealing. They encourage students to complete their records and then do the analysis. We do other things in agricultural education besides use the computer. But it's a great motivator!"

High school senior Leah Moen, president of the local Future Farmers of America, is a strong computer advocate. She took programming in the tenth grade and found it hard to understand. However, she says, "A year later, I saw how computers could help our farm and got interested right away. I learned to write a program to compare our farm's output with others'—and my father was really impressed." Leah's family has a fifteen-hundred-acre farm where they raise corn, oats, and hay as well as dairy cattle. "We use the computer to help determine which of the cattle are most productive. Then we feed the cows on the basis of how much they produce."

Leah's mother, Mary Jane Moen, is a strong supporter of the Ortonville computer program. She believes computers "give a good understanding of where the money goes and what it's used for." Leah's work "shows what the animals are eating and where to cut expenses." Mrs. Moen also appreciates the fact that Leah has used the school's computer for the last two years to maintain accurate records for the family's income taxes.

Fifteen-year-old Mike Danielson's family runs a five-hundred-acre farm where they raise corn, beans, oats, and wheat. Mike believes computers are changing the way farms are managed. When asked to name some specific computer services, he quickly runs through a series of programs that can help farmers with record keeping, such as inventory or cash-flow statements, then he lists the decision-making programs: hog planner, best crop per acre, and dairy planner. Mike says, "Before computers, farmers averaged things out in their minds. Now you can use the computer to think about different approaches and select the one which makes sense to you."

Angie Nolting, a sixteen-year-old, knows that the printouts she runs on the school computer are helping to operate her family's farm. "One of the programs helps us decide when to sell our market lambs so that we can get the most money out of them." Another program helped the family decide to put more money into feed next. "There are four kinds of feed: silage, hay, grain, and a high-protein concentrate," explains Angie. "Their costs vary—and we can calculate the impact of putting more money into each kind. We also can factor in the costs of shearing, heating the barn, and building depreciation. We saved a lot of money because of the computer and hope to do even better next year."

The students agree that using spreadsheets helps them in other classes. "It helps you learn to think logically," says Angie, whose parents believe she is more interested in math, and doing better, because of the "what if" programs. Angie's mother, Mary Ann, says, "This is one thing she really sunk her teeth in. It's done more for her math skills than some of the math classes she took."

Angie's success has encouraged her thirteen-year-old sister, Kim, who has asked the family to buy a pig that she will raise. "She's seen what Angie is doing, and wants to do the same thing."

Angie Nolting and Leah Moen intend to continue using computers. Angie hopes to study computers at a nearby vocational-technical institute, and she would like to have her own sheep farm some day, either in Minnesota or Montana. Leah has just received a "state farmer" award from the Future Farmers of America and agrees quietly when her teacher, Phillip Iverson, notes that the judges were very impressed with the program she wrote. She hopes to be able to buy a computer soon.

Angie says that everyone in this school "is really into computers," and she appears puzzled when asked whether male students are more interested in or have more access to the computers than female. "You don't hear anything like that here. Students help each other out all the time. It doesn't matter whether you are a guy or a girl—it's whether you know how to run the program."

The students' work has had an enormous impact on the community. Don Nolting, Angie's father, says there was "no talk at all about computers when I was growing up." But now, many of his neighbors are attending computer classes at the school, and some are buying computers for their farms. Agriculture education instructor Iverson notes that farmers taking the evening classes are welcome to use the school's computers for bookkeeping. Iverson and Nolting agree this has produced a real bond between the school and community. Nolting says his daughter's agricultural class "changed my view of school considerably. It helped me realize that school could teach my children things that would really help."

Iverson has several recommendations for communities that want to begin agricultural education computer projects:

1. "Begin with planning: what exactly will you be doing with the computer?
2. When you look at a machine, make sure it has enough memory to do the kind of work you want.
3. Don't be afraid to ask people what programs have been really useful, and which ones don't work so well. You can get a lot of money invested in something that won't fit your personal situation.
4. Remember that there are alternatives to purchasing your own computer. Schools should allow farmers to use their computers in conjunction with evening classes. A county agent may purchase computers that will be available on a loan, lease, or rental arrangement. And, of course, you may want to join with several other farmers and buy one together."

The Ortonville school computer projects unexpectedly produced several students who are master programmers. One of them, Curt Johnson, graduated but stayed on as a district employee to create new computer programs. Johnson has produced attendance, scheduling, grade recording, payroll, and finance programs. The school is particularly proud of the school lunch accounting software. Each student has a plastic card, which is scanned at lunch. The computer keeps track of how much each student eats and, at the end of each month, bills those families not eligible for free lunches.

Johnson isn't the only Ortonville graduate who has found computer-related employment. Several other graduates have worked in the local computer store, which was opened by the school's former math teacher. One indication of the school's effectiveness in promoting the use of computers on farms is that this town of twenty-two hundred people—more than a hundred miles from a metropolitan area—can support such a store!

The Ortonville experience is a classic home-school connection. Students see how some of their course work is instantly useful in life. The school can be of direct service to the community that supports it.

HELPING STUDENTS LEARN MORE ABOUT THEIR CITY

The Bernard Brown Elementary School in Hartford, Connecticut, is a long way from the high school in Ortonville, both in miles and mindset. While Ortonville is a quiet, relaxed small town, Hartford is a noisy, frenetic city. But students in the two locations do have one thing in common—an appreciation for the computer as a tool that can help people.

Several years ago, bright sixth graders in Hartford developed a computer game that can help other people learn about their city's educational resources and improve their map-reading, problem-solving, and language skills. The students created an educational program that applies the adventure game concept to an urban environment.

Daniel Barstow was an elementary school teacher working in the Hartford school district's bilingual program. Hartford schools have many students who speak Spanish in their homes, and the district recognized the need to help these youngsters learn English. Though some of the children don't speak English well, they are unusually bright, so the city developed special programs to challenge these students while helping them build language skills.

Barstow's responsibility was to help students increase their fluency in Spanish and English, and to provide learning challenges for those who were intellectually gifted. An avid computer user himself, he recognized the potential value of computers in furnishing creative, stimulating activities for students. He wrote a proposal to the Apple Computer Company, and the company responded by supplying the school with its first computer, software, and related equipment.

Barstow decided to apply adventure game principles to the learning process. Adventure was one of the first games played with computers. The program comes in many different forms, but in each one, players must move through various obstacles to reach a goal. Participants use creativity, memory, and ingenuity to "make it out alive" and, sometimes, find treasure.

The project began with Barstow taking students to the city's library. Later they visited the Children's Museum (in nearby West Hartford) and Wadsworth Atheneum, where they toured the art collections. They also talked with people in City Hall. The youngsters created large pictures of each trip. Each time they returned from an outing, Barstow encouraged his students to think of ways to assist people who wanted to know about an institution's resources. "Where can a student get information about the museum? What path would you take to get to the person with information? What would you pass on your way? What wrong turns are possible? What problems could develop? What's the best way to proceed?" As Barstow explains, "Each area was ripe for creative adventuring."

The next step was to think about ways to encourage exploration of the various facilities. Barstow recalls discussing a fish tank that students saw in the library. "The students decided to list three options: read about the fish, look at the fish, or touch the fish." Most students playing the game touched the fish. The game's response to that move: "Chomp, chomp. The fish were piranha. You just lost your hand. It's better to read about fish before touching them!" Students who selected the "read" option learned about the fish and their characteristics. Students who looked at the fish were encouraged to examine the creature's teeth and read about the fish before doing anything else.

In another section of the program, students walked to the entrance of a record room. They could talk with a librarian or go look at the records. Those selecting the second option found they'd somehow accidentally touched the records, which fall on the floor, making a mess and producing a request to leave the library.

Students created similar activities for many of the city's institutions. Barstow stresses that part of the program was helping players learn how to get from the front door of the school to the other buildings. "Often urban students don't go out of their own neighborhoods. We want them to feel comfortable throughout the city."

Next, students made a list of the pictures that would be needed to be a part of the program. They developed a sequence based on what they saw and experienced. Students drew illustrations with a Koala pad, a device that when connected to a computer produces colorful graphics.

Barstow says any school can do what he did. "The possibilities for creating your own adventure game are limitless. You can write an urban adventure that teaches about the resources in your own city or town. Or you can teach geography by writing an adventure that takes place in a different country. You could create an imaginary adventure land . . . or teach children about the human body by making a graphics adventure game to visually explore a computerized human body, with a heart that pumps and lungs that breathe." He says that students who are not gifted might not be as creative, and some youngsters obviously are more skilled at drawing than others. Nevertheless, he believes that the activities he pioneered are useful for a broad range of students.

Barstow has recommendations for people who want to try such projects:

1. Be sure to go on real adventures with kids. By actually going places, kids come up with ideas they would never have thought of while sitting at desks in their classroom.

2. Look for software that allows youngsters to create their own adventure games. Barstow mentions several: Spinnaker's Adventure Maker, CBS's Adventure Master, Scholastic's Story Tree, and Apple's Pilot or Super Pilot. The last was actually designed for teachers to write lessons but can be used to create the kind of activities described above.

3. Contact Barstow if you want to see the program he wrote. "Technically, it's in the public domain," he says.

4. Include a local or area map as part of the program. It's important to help youngsters learn how to get from one place to another.

5. Use various methods to allow students to choose their options. You might want to limit responses to numbers typed in from the keyboard. Other devices such as light pens, "joysticks," or "mouses" give the program more flexibility since they allow students to respond to questions, without typing, by pushing a button or drawing a line.

6. "Have fun" is Barstow's final, strong recommendation.

Barstow has received inquiries from people around the country, but doesn't know how many people have actually created their own games. He's eager to talk with people who want more information (and his address is listed in the Resources section of this book). Students gain a great deal from creating such programs, says Barstow. "They became experts about the Hartford Public Library and made dramatic gains in areas such as map reading and vocabulary in Spanish and English. They also learned a good deal about computers, planning and carrying out a complex educational activity." Barstow concludes that there are many ways to use computers with young people, but creating adventure games "is one of the most challenging and rewarding for everyone involved."

Dan Barstow is not the only educator who has used computers to help students teach each other. Eighth graders at Northern Iowa's Price Laboratory School in Cedar Falls, Iowa, worked with their teacher, Phil Nelson, and the school's computers to identify and draw attention to school problems. Youngsters in his class recently surveyed students, faculty, and administration regarding sex bias in the high school's athletic program and used the computer to tally the results of the survey. After some discussion of these results, the school made some changes, one of which was to buy more equipment for women's sports. The results of a similar study of the school lunch program led administrators to eliminate the most unpopular menus and offer popular meals more frequently.

The Iowa students used several commercially available programs. They enter their survey answers into the computer using a database program called PFS:File and then print out the results using a related program, PFS:Report (both from Software Publishing Corp.).

The teacher, Phil Nelson, says that the most important benefit to the students is that "they're able to obtain instant comparisons and analyses, and to look at their data in various ways" (Hunter, 1984, pp. 6-7). They also learn that many different interpretations of data are possible, depending on the way numbers are used. Young people who have learned to locate, organize, and analyze information will be more knowledgeable citizens. Beverly Hunter's work throughout this country shows that using computer data-management programs will stimulate teachers' and students' creativity. Hunter has helped educators in virtually every curriculum area create electronic libraries of information. She believes that "opportunities for student inquiry, problem-solving, and skill development are endless" (Hunter, 1985, p. 27).

Programs like these prepare young people for the twenty-first century. These students will be able to use computers to solve problems and share information, as well as to recognize the limitations of these powerful machines. The skills they learn will be invaluable in an advanced technological society.

PRACTICING A PARTNERSHIP WITH BUSINESS

Dan Roy says he had arguments with teachers almost every day in his old high school. But Project C.O.F.F.E.E. (Cooperative Federation of Educational Experiences), a nationally recognized alternative program in Oxford, Massachusetts, is "like a second home to me. I haven't been in any trouble here, and my grades are up quite a bit. To me, that is a big improvement."

Sixteen-year-old Donna Sneade, another student involved in the C.O.F.F.E.E. project, is studying word processing. She has worked in an office and likes to type and answer phones, and she hopes to get a job using word processing when she graduates from the program. She thinks the program's teachers are great. "You can talk to them like they are regular people."

The Oxford, Massachusetts, school district is similar to many other rural low- to moderate-income districts around the country. Its parents are interested in education and some of their children do well in school. But some students do not succeed. They are frustrated and often make it difficult for other students to learn and for some faculty to teach. Fortunately, administrators in Oxford decided in the late 1970s to respond creatively to the challenge of students who were not succeeding in their traditional high school. The district joined with a major computing company to create Project C.O.F.F.E.E.

The project began because "we weren't sure what to teach our kids about computers and other advanced technology," according to Dr. Frank Driscoll, Oxford school superintendent. Robert Richardson, director of a teacher center cosponsored by Oxford and several other school districts, agrees: "We wanted some help. We didn't even know the questions to ask." The district asked a number of advanced technology companies for help. One of them, Digital Equipment Corporation, a major manufacturer of business computers that has several facilities in Massachusetts, responded.

Digital is the second-largest employer in the Massachusetts/southern New Hampshire area, but hadn't had much previous contact with Oxford schools. None of its buildings are located in the school district. Its nearest facility is fifty-four miles away, and few of its employees live in the district. Oxford district staff members credit Digital with the willingness to look ahead: to recognize, as Driscoll puts it, that "they face a shortage of skilled workers. If they don't share their knowledge we won't be able to educate the kids. They will have to spend millions training employees to do anything significant. Forward-looking companies don't want that." Richardson says that Digital recognized that the school district's teacher center, which works with the project, could help train teachers and administrators from all over the region about the effective use of computers in education.

So Digital agreed to work with three school districts on a program to help students who are not succeeding.

The program has four integrated parts: basic skills instruction, occupational training, individual and group counseling, and physical education. Students attend classes four hours per day: two hours in basic skills, and two hours in hands-on occupational education. John Phillipo, former director of the project, says that the occupational training component is "the heart of the program, the focus of all the instruction the students receive" (Phillipo, p. 28).

Learning becomes meaningful for students as they see how they can apply what they learn. Two of the five occupational programs are related directly to the emerging electronics industry: computer maintenance/repair and word processing/spreadsheet analysis. Originally students received training in electronic assembly (putting together parts of computers). However, Digital officials pointed out that assembling skills were no longer in demand, but that word processing, database management, and spreadsheet analysis expertise were widely needed. Training shifted into those areas.

Another shift occurred when C.O.F.F.E.E. stopped teaching programming. Mike Fields, the project's director, says that Digital officials told him they did not need nearly as many programmers as they had a few years earlier. "We looked around and heard the same thing from other people. But all the projections we found said that computer technicians were going to be in short supply, along with word processing/data analysts. And most of our students weren't very interested in programming. So we shifted into those areas."

Dan Roy was one of those students. He took programming and data processing in the 1983-84 school year, but didn't enjoy it very much. "I like to work with my hands—to take things apart." The next year, Dan shifted into computer repair and maintenance and likes it much better.

Like Dan, Sue Berthiaume thought that she would like fixing computers better than "typing into them."

Sue is a seventeen-year-old student who left a private school to attend C.O.F.F.E.E. She is one of two young women who are joining eighteen young men in learning about computer repair. Sue says most of the guys don't bother her, though one told her she should let him take care of problems. "After all, you're a girl," he reminded her. But when Sue and several of the other students spent a week as interns at Digital, they found that most of the people in charge of the service center there were women. Sue says the guy who had teased her "was pretty quiet" after that experience. And seeing women in charge made her "feel like I had an edge—it encouraged me."

Fields says C.O.F.F.E.E. is trying to encourage students to take a broader, nontraditional view of work. Sixteen of the twenty students in the word-processing group are female; eighteen of the twenty students in the computer-repair program are male. "Our goal is to have at least twenty percent of the students in nontraditional groups," explains Fields. It helps to have a male program graduate working at Digital in word-processing/spreadsheet analysis. "He comes back to talk with students, and they listen to him. More models will help. But the culture's influence is quite strong."

The C.O.F.F.E.E program's staff deserves a great deal of credit, Fields says. "They understand and care about our students. I'm not sure every teacher could work with these young people, but our faculty could teach anywhere." Sixteen-year-old Erick Stevens says the C.O.F.F.E.E. teachers "don't talk like other teachers. They try to understand me and are willing to talk about my problems." Erick is learning to repair computers. He's the first person from his town of Douglas to attend the program. Since he started, several others have followed him.

The partnership between the Oxford public schools and Digital Equipment Corporation benefits the district, the corporation, and the students in many ways. Digital's staff trained some of Project C.O.F.F.E.E.'s teachers, as well as worked directly with students. The company donated materials and hosts students on field trips. Many students visited the company for one-day internships, during which they got a chance to practice skills developed in the project. Very popular with the students, these internships gave them a chance to talk with Digital employees and learn what skills would be needed to get a meaningful job. Driscoll (the Oxford school superintendent) says the value of equipment, software, and consulting time donated is more than $3 million.

But what does the corporation get out of this partnership? On a broad level, Digital has the opportunity to hire people who already have the critical skills its employees need. The company saves the expense of training employees who've graduated from the project. On a personal level, Digital employees report immense satisfaction from their involvement with young people. Dan Cooper, a consultant from Digital's education services department, describes it as the opportunity to help make "a spectacular difference in the lives of those kids."

Additional partnerships have developed as part of the program. In 1982, the owner of a local roller skating rink asked C.O.F.F.E.E. computer students to help catalog his record collection. Students wrote a computer program that sorted the records by artist and song title. Other C.O.F.F.E.E. students built a rack for the records. In return, the owner permits the program's students to skate free at the rink.

Another partnership involved computer repair. A number of Massachusetts school districts use Digital computers. Occasionally they need service. Project C.O.F.F.E.E. has repair contracts with several districts. Students know the machines they are working on are not toys—their work is real. People are counting on the quality of their work. The revenue generated by the service contracts helps pay for new equipment and student field trips.

C.O.F.F.E.E. has developed in many ways since 1979. Initially students came from three secondary schools. Six years later, students came from twelve secondary schools located in seven different districts. For its achievements, C.O.F.F.E.E. has received national recognition. The program was selected by the U.S. Department of Education as a "carefully evaluated, proven innovation worthy of national replication." And the President's Task Force on Private Sector Initiatives gave it a Presidential Commendation.

Perhaps more important than the awards the program has received are the differences it has made in the lives of youth. Students do not attend C.O.F.F.E.E. unless things are not going well at their traditional school (and sometimes at home and in their community). Donna Sneade speaks for many of the students when she says, "The regular high schools just have too many kids. People were always picking on someone. Here it's more like one big family."

The statistics *are* impressive. Superintendent Driscoll says eighty-four percent of the students who have entered the program successfully complete it. Forty percent of the approximately one-hundred-and fifty students who've attended the program have returned to their own high school and graduated. Twenty-five of the students have graduated from C.O.F.F.E.E. itself, and thirteen of them are working in advanced technology fields. Another six C.O.F.F.E.E. graduates are in the Armed Forces, all of them using skills learned at the program's computer center. Several graduates are attending post-secondary programs in advanced technology areas.

In his thirty-seven years as an educator, Frank Driscoll has seen many programs for dropouts, but few that worked well. "It's a tough group. But this is one good answer to educating these kids. Sometimes they're rascals . . . sometimes down-and-outers. But they do want to learn, if we can reach them. This program does."

Digital's Mike Odom agrees that the cooperation between his company and Oxford has been a real success. He calls it "the nicest working experience I've ever had." Odom says myths about schools and businesses have been destroyed. Business people and educators have "stopped thinking about them and us, and started thinking about all of us." Before the project, some Digital executives thought they could do a much better job of running schools than educators. "Now they understand constraints under which schools work. It's clear that simplistic solutions won't work," reports Odom. However, Digital recognizes that cooperation can be mutually beneficial. "We're very pleased—delighted to see changes in the lives of kids."

Odom makes the following suggestions to organizations wishing to establish a cooperative relationship:

1. Begin by sitting down informally to talk about mutual needs. "The term 'C.O.F.F.E.E.' is appropriate, because we began our discussions over a cup of coffee."

2. Pick areas of mutual interest. Projects are much more likely to grow and continue if they matter to everyone involved.

3. Negotiate, and decide on one area in which to begin. "Don't try to do too much, too fast. Establish one real success and others will develop rapidly."

4. Take the idea of real change seriously on both sides. Otherwise, the project will simply involve donation of some equipment or dollars, and not much will really change. "It will be good PR—but the project won't have much impact."

5. Remember that one thing will lead to another. Try to expand the number of people involved from each participating institution. That way, projects won't die when one key person, such as a principal, teacher, superintendent, supervisor, or manager, leaves. "Inevitably some people will change jobs or responsibilities. The strongest projects will involve many people."

6. Accept the fact that cooperation may lead to areas no one imagined in the beginning. Don't insist that everything be completely planned at the start, or you will close off possibilities that may be more important, effective, and worthwhile than those with which you started.

Most of the C.O.F.F.E.E. students don't think in global terms about corporate-school partnerships. They know that this program works for them. Students report varying reactions from their friends. Sue Berthiaume recalls that when one girl found out where Sue was going to school, she teased, "Do you have sugar and cream with C.O.F.F.E.E.?" But more recently, she said, "Some of them wonder if they should get into the program. They can see I'm learning important, valuable skills." Erick Stevens, having convinced others from his town to attend, says flatly, "There's no better school." Perhaps Dan Roy put it best: "C.O.F.F.E.E. is a terrific place for people who can't make it through a regular high school but want to learn. It's like a second chance. It's helped me take some big steps toward success."

CIRCUMVENTING HANDICAPS: MAKING A DIFFERENCE IN THE LIVES OF KIDS

Budd and Delores Hagen, who were mentioned in an earlier chapter, were extremely concerned about their son Marc's transition from elementary to junior high school. As Delores explained, "He had done all right in elementary school, but things were just not working out at the local junior high in Henderson, Minnesota." The Hagens' concern led to dramatic educational improvements for their son and for other disabled youth throughout North America.

Marc is deaf. His speech was not as good as that of most other youngsters his age, and they were starting to let him know it. Other students hadn't bothered him much in elementary school, but a good deal of teasing had developed in the junior high. For the first time, he was not eager to attend school. The Hagens decided to talk with Marc's teachers to see what could be done. Delores recalls, "They didn't have many ideas. But one of them said, 'Well, we just got these computers. Do you think they could help?' We'd been reading about computers and thought, 'This is the time to act.'"

The Hagens did a good deal of reading and discovered that many products were available to help disabled youngsters. Budd observes, "Most of these products were not designed with handicapped people in mind. Word-processing programs were created to improve business office efficiency. But our son found he could write much better with a word processor. Modems (devices that link computers via telephone lines) were created to permit business computers to communicate with each other. But Marc found he could communicate much better by having electronic conversations. These devices gave him much greater self-confidence. And everything started getting better."

But the Hagens found there was not a good central place to get information about use of computers for disabled people. So they changed businesses. They had been putting out a newspaper for skiers. They decided to put out a new newspaper: a publication devoted to showing parents and educators how to use computers to help handicapped people. They hoped that people in Minnesota would be interested, and perhaps people in the region. "But by our fourth issue, in less than a year, we had subscribers in each of the states and Canadian provinces, and about twenty-five other countries," Budd recalls. And it's been remarkable what's happened since.

The Hagens approached the local school district about using vacant space in the high school. Fortunately, district officials agreed to a cooperative project. The district provides space, and the Hagens provide training for district staff, plus access to the computer lab they've acquired. The lab now has more than twenty

Apples, plus a number of other machines and equipment specifically geared to the needs of handicapped people. Budd says, "It's a nice arrangement. Henderson seems to love it—we love it."

Using their lab and office as a base, the Hagens have worked with educators and parents throughout North America. They began when a woman from Philadelphia showed up on their porch, asking for help. Now the world is starting to discover them.

The Hagens say computers provide access for handicapped people that they might otherwise be unable to approach. Budd explains, "First, their special needs can be met. Then the computer can help meet needs every person has: for communication, learning, a job and recreation." Budd says parents and teachers of handicapped youngsters should adopt an attitude of "it's probably possible." They should not give up hope, regardless of what they've been told about their child's limitations. He says many traditional diagnoses are not accurate and he can cite a number of examples, including one in a nearby community. A little boy was born with only half a normal brain. Doctors said he would never be able to communicate much with other people. Now, with the help of a computer and special keyboard, "he's a flaming conversationalist. He defies all the things people said he couldn't do."

Computers create many new opportunities for handicapped children. A creative Arizona teacher has found that, with an assist from the school's computer, her learning and emotionally disabled children could become resources to other children. Miriam Furst became intrigued with the possibilities of helping her third through eighth graders become "facilitators of learning" (instead of always being the recipients of assistance). She helped her youngsters learn to write programs to teach reading, math, spelling, science, and driver education to themselves and others. The students used both the programming and graphic capabilities of computers to create unusual and often creative learning games. The results were dramatic! Furst's students shared the game with fellow students, other teachers, and their parents, and the young people, so used to failure and rejection, got approval and praise. The "normal" students began to ask for the chance to work with and learn from the "handicapped" students.

Such stories encourage, but do not surprise Budd and Delores Hagen. Delores has written a book about how to help handicapped children by using computers. Though the book was directed to parents like herself, it's been adopted by a number of colleges and universities. They are using it with students who are preparing to work with such youngsters. Hagen has several recommendations for bringing together computers and a handicapped or disabled person:

1. Establish what the child's handicap really is. This requires permitting the child to try out various kinds of computers and related equipment. "People may think that a child can't communicate with other people. But the child may just not be able to speak. So helping the child learn to type a message on a computer will permit communication. Or a child may not be able to hear. A computer can help the youngster learn to read." By bringing together children and computers, Hagen says she is often able to show parents and educators how handicaps can be circumvented.

2. Develop the youngster's ability to interact with and control an environment. "So many handicapped children feel defeated. We must help convince them that they can learn and communicate. Once this happens, progress often comes at an astonishing rate."

3. Permit students to show you their preferred learning style. "Everyone has a special, distinct way to learn which is a bit different from others. What works well with one disabled child may be totally inappropriate for another, even though they appear to have identical disabilities," Delores insists. "Computers will help teach parents and educators a great deal about

children, if we listen and watch, if we don't go in with pat answers."

4. Don't limit your search for appropriate materials and equipment to those that have been developed specifically for education, or for handicapped people. One of the most important devices for some handicapped people is the speech-synthesizer. This device permits computers to talk to people. And yet, Budd points out, the device was originally developed to enhance computer games.

There are many consultants in education, but most of them are former teachers or administrators. Educators traditionally have not had high expectations of "experts." Teachers and administrators don't want to hear a lot of theory; educators want practical ideas about how to help people. Budd and Delores Hagen have passed tough tests with teachers—they've been asked to come back again and again. "They know we won't talk theory, we'll talk about kids. And we won't talk about why something can't be done. We'll help them use computers to develop ways of getting around those disabilities and handicaps." Delores concludes, "People are lying in bed, unable to take care of themselves. Many of them feel like useless burdens when they could be using computers and living again."

Many Americans are concerned about the quality of their schools. Although enrollments are declining in many places, costs continue to increase. When citizens have strong evidence of students learning and of the effective use of their tax dollars—as in Folsum, Ortonville, Hartford, and Oxford—the gap between them and the schools closes. Trust increases. As Don Nolting, a farmer in rural Ortonville, explains, "It really brings the two minds together." In these towns, creative, thoughtful people are using computers to help solve significant problems.

10

ENCOURAGING THE USE
OF WORD PROCESSING

Chapter 9 showed that some teachers and students are making creative, educational use of available software to solve real-world problems. For them, it is demonstrably not true that there is no good educational software. In this chapter I want to look at other teachers who are using available software to teach an important skill. Various studies, along with popular perception, say that many students are not learning to write well in our schools. Word processing—one of the most powerful and accessible computer applications—can encourage and assist the development of writing skills.

Word processing provides four main capabilities:
- the ability to instantaneously correct spelling or grammatical errors;
- the ability to insert or delete words, phrases, paragraphs, or pages into a document;
- the ability to quickly print what has been written; and
- the ability to provide teachers with clear copies of students' writing.

Word processing does *not* help people learn to make an outline, improve their spelling, or understand rules of grammar and punctuation. But its power does help writers get their ideas down quickly, and then make revisions easily and rapidly. Children as young as eight or nine are learning how to do word processing, and older students, like eighteen-year-old Carrie Clinton, are ecstatic about writing on a computer. "I love it," she says. "It's much easier to get your work in on time. You don't have to carry papers around. And so you don't lose them."

For three years, high school teachers in the Minneapolis suburb of Lakeville have been using word processors to teach writing. The Lakeville program has grown from two computers being used by thirteen Practical English students to twenty-eight computers used by 425 senior high students. Ed Mako, an English teacher at the school, began by using word processing with eleventh grade students whose previous record in writing was "miserable." In a year, Mako saw dramatic changes in three areas: "the students' willingness to write, their willingness to share with each other, and their willingness to share with their teacher." Encouraged by dramatic improvements with students who had known so little success in the past, Mako convinced the school district to establish a lab with twenty-five computers and several printers, where the machines would be used only for word processing.

Mako says the word-processing laboratory has made a major difference in the school. "English teachers don't have to fight with math and science teachers for the computers," he says. "Teachers from other schools tell me how frustrating it is to argue about word processing versus programming and other uses. We don't have that problem—different computers are used for various applications. The availablity of machines has made all the difference in this school." Some of the nine high school English teachers initially were skeptical about the use of computers to improve students' writing. But today, Mako reports, all of the instructors support word processing. They all are using it with some of their classes. The school's goal is that by the end of the 1985-86 school year, all of its students will use word processing to revise their papers.

English Department chair Wayne Daugherty supports the word-processing lab. He describes himself as "very hesitant" about the whole idea in the beginning, but "much more optimistic" now. Second-year teacher Tim Weier shared Daugherty's skepticism. "I was a stick in the mud, but now I'm convinced. It's easier to get assignments in from students who did not like writing. And their attitude is so much better. Their self-esteem is way up." He points to his grade book. "Before we started using the word processor, I was pleased to get papers from two-thirds of the students in the Practical English class. Now I get them from almost everyone— every time." Weier says that before the class began using computers, the students would count every word in their essays when he assigned 150 words. "Now they come up to me and ask if it's OK if they write more than 150 words!" Weier says his relationship with students has changed. "I get along better with them in the lab than in class. The computers make me a resource to the students. I can get to them quicker."

Senior teacher Denny Corcoran agrees with Weier about changes in slower students' attitudes toward writing. "They're so impressed with what they can accomplish in terms of quality and length. I'm pleased for them." Corcoran says the average and bright students also like working with computers. He wonders "if the novelty will wear off . . . but it certainly hasn't so far."

In order to make the most effective use of word processing, people should know how to type. Lakeville high school students spend two hours learning the fundamentals of typing. Their English teachers show them where to place their fingers on the keyboard and help them practice typing. Students then use a commercially produced word-processing package called Word-Handler. Students using word processing increased the use of simple and compound sentences and descriptive phrases much more than students revising in longhand. Word-processing students also had fewer spelling and mechanical errors. Teachers also noticed that students using word processors spent more time helping each other and working with the teacher on revisions, cutting the time required to correct papers. This meant that computers helped improve students' ability to write and helped the teachers involved make better use of their time. One teacher told Mako that before word processing, he needed about nine hours to comment on each class assignment in a creative writing class. That time has been cut to three-and-a-half hours because word processing has eliminated lots of mistakes and makes it easy to produce clear copies of a student's writing.

Word processing has not solved all the students' problems with writing, however. Seventeen-year-old Kelly Swanson says it's easier to fix mistakes using the computer, but she's "not sure it actually improves my writing." And word processing can bring a new set of problems. One senior discovered that her five-page essay, due the following day, had somehow become erased from the floppy disk. She needed to write only one paragraph to finish the essay and was quite upset. "I know what I'll be doing during Christmas vacation," she murmured to her friends. Her teacher later said that such events are unusual, but that it's important to have a backup copy of what a student has written.

Despite any problems, Mako and the other English teachers believe word processing is extremely worthwhile. Says Mako, "This is my twenty-sixth year in teaching. I'm starting to think that finally, with the help of these machines, almost all our students will learn to enjoy writing. And good writing is the product of good thinking."

Lakeville is using word processing in its secondary schools, but some educators think students can learn to use a computer keyboard even earlier. Creative elementary school teachers are developing new ways to teach typing, and to encourage writing via word processing. One such teacher, who has won national awards for her work, is Judy Anderson.

Anderson's first commitment is to her students at East Consolidated Elementary School (ECON) in St. Paul,

Minnesota. Now in her fifteenth year of teaching, she directs the school's computer room, which holds twenty-six Apples. Working closely with the principal, Dr. Bill Schrankler, and the other members of the staff, Anderson has developed a program in which each of ECON's students spends at least thirty minutes a day, every other day, on a computer. Located in an old section of the city, the school has seven hundred students, grades K-6. About thirty percent of the students are Hmong, black, Hispanic, and Native American.

The school's computers are used for three major purposes: word processing, LOGO, and modified drill-and-practice. Anderson uses a commercial word processing package with fourth through sixth graders. She's written a version of LOGO called EZ LOGO (for which she received an award from Minnesota Educational Computing Corporation). She works constantly with other building staff members to tie computer use into their classroom goals and lessons. Rather than seeing computers as objects to study in and of themselves, Anderson views computers as tools to support and enrich the entire curriculum.

Principal Bill Schrankler credits Anderson's willingness to work closely with other staff as a key reason why other teachers accepted his proposal to create a computer resource position. Schrankler determined several years ago that it would not be possible to obtain an extra position for his staff. He decided that if Anderson's class of twenty-six students could be distributed to other teachers, she could be in the computer lab full-time, working with students from throughout the school. He talked with faculty members about the possibility of increasing their class sizes by several students, the trade-off being that their classes could work in the computer lab several times per week. Shrankler says he worked for and achieved an informal consensus among the staff supporting the establishment of a person in charge of the computer lab.

Judy Anderson arrives at the school about 7:00 a.m. and spends an hour making sure the computers are working and checking materials for the many groups she sees each day. She prepares a variety of overhead transparencies and handouts for the students. These include pictures of the keyboard, explanations of how to take care of floppy disks, and samples of figures constructed using LOGO.

Some early morning hours are spent working on various computer programs. Anderson constantly writes new programs, or modifies existing ones for use at the school. She also reviews new programs to decide which ones she will recommend for purchase. She has established files enabling classroom teachers to keep track of their students' attendance, then their progress in reading and math. Each of the seven hundred ECON students has a record, which must be constantly updated. In the hour before classes begin, other teachers often stop by to discuss what their students will be doing in the lab that day, or to pick up reports summarizing their students' growth in reading and math.

Between 8:00 and 2:30, Anderson works with about 330 kids in half-hour segments. Each classroom teacher comes to the lab with the students, to assist and learn along with them. In most cases, the teacher has prepared students for what they will be doing in the lab. Anderson thinks this is a better arrangement than the way she started. Two years ago the lab opened with classroom teachers sending half their students to the lab and keeping the other half in the classroom. Anderson says, "With two of us in the lab, we all gain. The other teachers get experience with computers; they can relate classroom and computer work, and of course, two people can respond to questions more quickly than one!"

Anderson has worked hard to adapt word processing for elementary-age students. She is a strong writing advocate and sees daily examples of increased enthusiasm for composition because ECON's youngsters can use computers to create and modify their paragraphs and stories. Anderson likes the Apple Writer program for school use. She has created note card-size instructions that summarize the major commands. She's also designed lessons to explain major features of the word-processing program, such as entering, revising, saving, and printing text.

Introducing word processing into elementary schools created pressure for students to learn keyboard skills. Judy Anderson uses a three-step process to teach typing.

First, she goes to classrooms with enough paper copies of the computer's keyboard so that each student can have one. The paper copy is exactly the same size as the computer keyboard. She explains the keyboard and then has the students color the "home" keys: *a, s, d, f, g, h, j, k,* and *l.* Then she has the students put their fingers on those keys, just as they would on the computer. Anderson has prepared a laminated card for each student that shows the keyboard, and has the home keys colored yellow. Anderson (and later the classroom teacher) has the students practice pressing the keys, an experience that makes them more familiar with the location of the keys and more comfortable with the typing process. Classroom teachers have worked out a system so that pairs of students can drill each other for five to ten minutes during the day, making it a good activity when a lesson runs a few minutes short or while students are waiting for lunch.

The second step in teaching keyboard skills is to bring the students into the computer lab. Students are taught to turn on the computer and then put their fingers on the home keys. They type "home" so that the cursor goes to the top of the screen. Then they begin the keyboard drill that they've used in the classroom. Now, however, the letters they type appear before them on a monitor. Anderson always looks forward to the first day a group of students use the computers. "It's like magic for them—'look what happened,' they shout and giggle." Anderson continues the drill during that first session. As they did with the paper keyboards, students share a computer, and drill each other. Anderson finds she must encourage students to keep their eyes up, looking at the screen, rather than down, looking at the keyboard.

The third step in teaching the use of the keyboard is to have students play a game that encourages them to learn the various letters. After reviewing many such programs, Anderson selected MasterType (by Scarborough Software). She likes a number of the program's features, including its ability to individualize speed and give students more practice on letters they are missing.

Anderson notes, "Sometimes it takes another year or two for the students to develop the physical dexterity or interest in using the computers. We have a few second graders who prefer not to use the computer to write. But virtually all of the fourth through sixth graders love it!"

Several university professors have visited the school to learn how Anderson teaches elementary students to type. "Some of them shake their heads, saying they just didn't think it was possible," she says.

Two-thirty brings the end of the school day for her students, but it's often just the end of one kind of teaching for Judy Anderson. Three days per week she has an after-school workshop. She and the principal arranged a series on word processing that about half of ECON's staff attended. The school district computer coordinator and assistant superintendent have arranged for her to teach several districtwide in-service courses—one on word processing for elementary and secondary teachers, the other on administrative uses of the microcomputer. The assistant superintendent also asked Anderson to demonstrate word-processing possibilities to district curriculum specialists. She teaches evening courses for a local university and Saturday morning courses at the St. Paul Science Museum.

Anderson credits a colleague at ECON for teaching her about classroom computer applications. "When I got to the school, Dave Thofern and I worked together. He taught me a great deal and helped the entire faculty understand advantages of having a centralized computer lab rather than one or two computers per classroom."

Anderson is grateful for the opportunity to be a computer classroom coordinator. It's allowed her to grow: to work with students ages five through twelve, rather than just the fifth and sixth graders she began teaching fifteen years ago; to think about staff development, curriculum, and other technologies. Most important, she believes that her job "gives me an opportunity to make use of talents and interests that a typical classroom position doesn't tap. A computer coordinator shouldn't be the only one in a school who knows about computers," she explains. "In fact, part of my job is to increase awareness and understanding among staff and parents. The computer specialist, first and foremost, should have a broad view of curriculum. It's not nearly enough to know about technical features of a machine. Too often the computer is viewed as the answer to *everything*. It won't be the answer to *anything* if those using it don't have a broad view of how children learn and what curriculum goals and objectives a school has."

Anderson cites teaching seven-year-olds to type as an example of knowledge an elementary teacher has that a technically trained person might not possess. "We know about the importance of making it fun. We also know that it's important to remind kids not to look at the keyboard, and to keep their fingers on the home keys. People who spend time around kids know how they'll react to new experiences, and can anticipate problems. That's why I encourage outstanding teachers to learn about computers. Computers are just one more tool to help youngsters gain basic and applied skills and see themselves as competent people."

She has strong feelings about centralizing versus dispersing computers. "A lab with at least thirteen to fifteen computers allows an entire class to work together, at the same time (figuring twenty-six to thirty students per class). The computer becomes a tool to help them all achieve certain class objectives. Often when you have only one to two computers per room, the computer is used as a reward. In some cases where a classroom has only a couple computers, aggressive kids get more access to the computer, and quiet kids who could gain a great deal have fewer opportunities. Monitoring the use of a classroom's computer can be just one more task for already overworked teachers.

"However, a computer lab won't work well if you don't have someone who knows both the kids and machines well," she continues. "If a school has a lab without some really knowledgeable people, the machines probably will be underused—most often for drill-and-practice, since it's the easiest to just plug into the machine.

"Labs require a great deal of cooperation and coordination among teachers. The classroom teachers and I talk before or after school or during their breaks about what we'll do when their class comes in. They tell me about kids who may need particular attention and encouragement. In the beginning, some teachers seemed to regard scheduling time in the lab as one more complication. Now most of them see it as a powerful tool which will help them accomplish their goals for the class."

Anderson stresses that "the classroom teacher's enthusiasm, high student expectation and method of teaching writing as a process are the keys" to the success of a computer lab, and adds, "A computer lab is also very valuable for staff development. We can be ready for an in-service five minutes after the kids go home. If the computers were in rooms, we'd have to move them around a lot (or perhaps set up a district center where teachers go for in-service). This way our school's computers can be used easily for both students and faculty."

Ed Mako at Lakeville agrees with Anderson about the value of a computer lab. As part of his graduate work, he has reviewed research on the use of computers to teach writing. "In most of the studies, teachers had one or two computers in their room. You can hear their frustration coming out in their articles. I think it's defeating the whole purpose of improving all students' writing to disperse computers, one or two in a classroom." Mako says that spreading the computers makes it unlikely that all students will get a chance to use them. "In much of the research I've read, teachers talk about how the better students are the ones who use the computers (when there are just one or two in a room). The less able students think it's too hard to learn. These kids just won't demand a turn. They'll avoid it, figuring it's one more thing they're 'too dumb to learn.'"

Both Mako and Anderson are pleased that their schools are using the computer lab approach. They find that parents are happy with what's being done with computers. Both report that parents tell them, "Our kids are much more enthusiastic about writing." Some parents call to ask which computers they should buy for their children.

Mako and Anderson salute the teachers with whom they work. There was initial skepticism about some of their proposals, but there was also an openness to try and a willingness to accept new ideas that clearly helped students. Many of their fellow teachers ask about ways to use computer capabilities in other areas. "We have a certain credibility," says Anderson. "They know we understand their situation, and that I'll try to make practical, specific suggestions."

Mako credits his school's principal with listening to and supporting him (and resisting the push from some teachers to reserve most of the school's computers for programming instruction). Anderson agrees: "My school—the principal, staff, kids and parents—is just great."

However, it's also important to note what has happened recently. After several years as a computer lab coordinator, Anderson took a sabbatical from the school district. "I wanted to get an administrative certificate.

The way things are set up now, you have to be an administrator to have a broader impact." After she took her leave, the district decided to create several new staff positions. Those selected are responsible for helping teachers in a number of schools design effective programs using computers. This is a good example of a district adapting its personnel policies so that everybody wins. Outstanding teachers have new career opportunities, and the district and its students retain their teachers' expertise.

Pioneering teachers such as St. Paul's Judy Anderson and Lakeville's Ed Mako point the way for significant developments in learning, particularly in using word processing in schools. While too modest to admit it, they are models for others. Their efforts ought to force educators to examine how learning occurs, and to find some of the most exciting answers not in universities and advanced institutes, but in the schools themselves.

11

BUYING EDUCATIONAL
SOFTWARE

The last two chapters show how computers can be used
to solve problems and improve basic skills with software that wasn't designed specifically for schools. The
software described, however, is not the only valuable
material available for educational use. This chapter
offers examples of other kinds of software worth considering and advice on how to select it. People planning to
purchase material for their computer must either do a
good deal of research or waste money.

Unfortunately, the software customer needs to be
aware of a number of negative qualities of educational
software currently on the market. Educational software

- may not run on the machine you own. Computers,
  unlike stereo systems, are not yet completely standardized. A record will run on any phonograph system, but the disk for an Apple will not operate on an
  IBM, Atari, Commodore, Radio Shack, Texas Instrument, or Epson computer. The buyer must make sure
  the software will run on a particular machine. Otherwise, the disk will be useless;
- is often of poor quality. The Educational Products
  Information Exchange (EPIE) Institute, a nonprofit
  group based at Teachers College, Columbia University, is widely regarded as one of the most informed
  and reputable organizations reviewing educational
  software. EPIE has identified more than seven thousand educational software packages and conducted

detailed evaluations of several hundred of the most popular. The results? Executive Director Kenneth Komoski says, "Only about one out of twenty has been judged good enough to be placed in the 'Highly Recommended' category . . . while more than half have been judged not worth recommending to educators or parents" (Komoski, p. 247). Jack Kleinmann of the National Foundation for the Improvement of Education agrees, "There's a lot of junk out there" (Bonner, p. 69);

- often bores youngsters after they use it a few times;
- rarely makes sophisticated use of computer capabilities;
- is often overpriced;
- is sometimes in direct conflict with a family's values;
- sometimes does not include clear directions about how to use it;
- may include vocabulary that is either too easy or too difficult for the people for whom it is intended;
- sometimes cannot be returned, despite the fact that there are problems with the disk; and
- may have been reviewed by someone who has been paid by its producer to say good things about it.

At the same time, software is sometimes superb—remarkably creative and effective. Some of the best software is produced by companies founded by former teachers or others who work closely with teachers. Many of these companies are not bound or influenced by the traditional textbook attitude that produced books that students generally do not read unless they have to. Traditional textbooks often operate on a read-the-chapter-and-answer-the-questions-at-the-end mentality. The software that textbook companies produce often reflects this approach to learning. The more creative software is challenging, stimulating, and, I think, much more effective.

My review of software supports these conclusions. Many packages consist of reading a section and answering questions. The computer may ask a student's name and compliment her or him on doing well. It may flash a few pictures or light rockets. But many youngsters grow tired of this after a few lessons. As one teacher told the *New York Times*, "The idea was that kids would learn more if they could shoot down airplanes by multiplying numbers. But drill and practice didn't work. Students don't like to practice their numbers on a computer any more than they like to do it on paper." Another teacher commented that most of the software she examines "turns out to be something you could do with an overhead projector" (Fiske, p. 34).

Taking both the negative and the positive qualities of educational software into account, it follows that you should buy software

- after ensuring that it will run on the computer that's available;
- after considering the interests, abilities, needs, and sophistication of the potential user;
- that takes advantage of the computer's sophisticated capabilities;
- that will encourage youngsters to develop basic and applied skills;
- that will be used more than a few times;
- that helps youngsters understand ways in which the computer can be a powerful tool, something like a hammer, a saw, or an automobile;
- that includes clear, comprehensive descriptions on how to use it;
- that uses vocabulary appropriate to the students for whom it is intended;
- after determining that the store selling it or the company producing it will take it back if there are problems; and
- after reading reviews or talking with other computer users who convince you that the program will be worth purchasing.

Fortunately, some stores, such as B. Dalton, are now permitting customers to preview software before they buy it. This is a wonderful opportunity that should be used, not abused. If consumers support retailers who permit review, the practice will spread. If the policy is abused, it will be discontinued and everyone will lose.

As with other merchandise, software can be bought directly by mail. Many of the computing magazines listed in the Resources section of this book include advertisements from mail-order houses that offer discounts on software. Consumers who buy from these places take the same risks as with other kinds of mail-order houses. Some companies are reputable; others aren't. Some accept returns of defective merchandise; others don't. Some will be around in a month if you have a problem; others won't. A good software store will carry a much broader selection than many "order by mail" firms, and will offer the opportunity to examine software before purchasing. However, people in small towns and rural areas often do not have access to a software store and must purchase many things from catalogs.

Educational software falls into a half-dozen or so basic categories. I would like to examine these categories and look at some of the specific programs available from manufacturers. When reading about the particular products listed here, however, do keep three things in mind: (1) software preferences differ from one person to another, so any recommendations must be reviewed in light of the values and interests of the person who will be using the computer; (2) thousands of programs have been produced for use in homes and schools, and the products I mention are not the only high-quality ones available; and (3) I am on the board of the Minnesota Educational Computing Corporation, an organization that, among other things, produces software for school and home use. I have tried to be clear, honest, and fair, but I am not neutral.

TYPING PROGRAMS

Parents who have purchased computers for their homes should encourage their children to learn how to type. Typing permits much more efficient use of a computer. It's ironic that people buy a machine to help them be more productive, and then fail to learn a simple skill that permits them to make more productive use of the machine. It's something like learning to drive only on side streets, but resisting learning how to drive on freeways. You'll do all right on quiet city streets, but you won't get as much use from the car as you would if you were able to drive cross-country.

There are several ways to learn to type. One is to take a course in school. Most secondary schools offer such courses, during the regular academic year and during summer programs. Some school districts are beginning to offer typing as part of summer elementary computer courses or during evening community education classes.

Some parents are buying software that promises to teach children and adults how to type, but not all professional educators think it wise to rely exclusively on a software package to help young people learn to type. Some people will be able to teach themselves to type by practicing with a book, or using a tutorial computer program. The most effective learning appears to occur when the student works with a person who knows how to type and has experience helping others learn, and uses computer programs as a supplement.

There are two major kinds of programs available to help improve one's typing. The first is instructional: "Here's where to put your fingers, here are some exercises to help you improve your fingering." The second is drill: programs to encourage and assist in building typing speed.

Several programs of the "fingering" variety are available, with more coming out every month. Two examples are Typing Tutor III, published by Simon and

Schuster, and MicroType, published by South-Western. The Typing Tutor program has been revised several times, improving with each update. It is probably the bestselling product in the field. MicroType is geared for nine- to thirteen-year-old students, though it can be used by people of any age.

Many programs are available to help youngsters increase the speed of their typing. MasterType, by Scarborough Software, is the best selling typing "drill" program. It helps build speed, can be set at different rates, and shows how many mistakes a user made—all valuable characteristics. (The way MasterType encourages the development of speed is worth describing: typists "zap" space people before they are able to destroy a space ship. Some parents object to this, but elementary teachers who have used it with their students report no major increase in violence among their students. However, it's difficult to measure long-term effects of such a program.)

The term *keyboarding* sometimes is used to differentiate between using a regular typewriter and a computer keyboard. People who use a typewriter must know how to set margins, insert paper, determine where the bottom of the page is, and learn other skills not generally needed in using a computer. Computers have a few keys that are not found on typewriters. These computer keys vary in function, but generally enhance the computer's power to do something quickly (such as tabulate, print, or save information).

It's much easier to use a word-processing program if you know how to type. That means both knowing where to put your fingers and developing speed.

Consider buying a word-processing package for any computer-user over age eight. Most parents want their children to learn to write clearly, coherently, and accurately, and most schools require some writing. Solid research cited earlier shows that many young people are more enthusiastic about writing and spend more time revising and polishing their work when they use a computer's word-processing capabilities. Word processing eliminates the drudgery of recopying a paper and makes the correction process much more fun. In general, if an adult can figure out a word-processing program, so can a young person over the age of ten.

Which word-processing package should be bought? Many parents already have word-processing software that came with their computer. If you happen not to, there are a number of less expensive word-processing programs intended primarily for use with young people. One excellent example is Magic Slate, by Sunburst, which is very good for children ages five to eight. This program has several outstanding features. It can show letters of three different sizes, the largest of which are approximately four times the size of the print on this page, making them much easier to read. As the children get older, the letters can be reduced to about twice the size of those on this page and then, if a family has a computer with enough power, Magic Slate will provide letters about the size of those on this page. Unlike some other programs (including the one I'm using), Sunburst's word-processing program permits users to see "on the screen" exactly how what they've written will appear when it is printed. It also is easy to learn and use and has many features of more expensive programs.

LOGICAL THINKING PROGRAMS
Another worthwhile kind of program helps young people learn to think through problems logically. Some of the most popular and exemplary software is available in this category. Sunburst Software has won numerous awards for its Factory program, in which users must identify machines that will create a product with combinations of holes, stripes, and shapes. Young people can design their own product or try to figure out the steps required to make a product that they see pictured. The program is designed with different levels of difficulty

and it can challenge anyone from ages five through adult.

One of the best-selling, most highly praised problem-solving pieces of software is Rocky's Boots, from Learning Games. People using the program try to build a series of "logic machines." If successful, they score points and win the game. Young people who've used this program report it to be "extremely challenging, but lots of fun."

PROJECT PROGRAMS

Some software programs can be used as tools with which to construct projects. Two excellent "tool packages" are Print Shop, by Broderbund, and The Newsroom, by Springboard Software. Print Shop lets young people design and create their own banners, stationery, and signs. Recently, several teenagers at the McKinley Alternative School in Fairbanks, Alaska, created their own business using this program with the school's computer and printer. They began by producing individualized stationery for students. Then staff members and parents heard about the product and placed a number of orders. Fourteen-year-old Jim Jernstrom, who is in charge of the operation, says, "It's neat. It gives me something to do before school and at lunch time." The Newsroom allows youngsters and adults to publish their own newspapers by helping them create banners, stories, and pictures and then "lay out" the pages. It even lets them send the final product over telephone lines, if they have the right equipment. Both programs have many uses.

SIMULATION PROGRAMS

Simulations use the computer's ability to put young people in unfamiliar situations. The best educational simulations are both fun and instructive. Elementary-age students (ages seven to ten) enjoy Marketplace, from the Minnesota Educational Computing Corporation. The most popular of the three programs on this disk is Sell Lemonade, which lets players get a feel for operating a lemonade stand. They must decide how much lemonade to make, how much to spend on advertising, and how much to charge per glass. They learn that the weather has an impact, and they encounter unexpected price increases. Players go through a week's business, quickly learning basic capitalism. The most effective use of the simulation is with young people who are preparing to operate their own business. Several eight- to ten-year-old users explained what using this program meant to them: "It showed me the steps to go through in figuring out how much to charge." "It helped me be prepared for rain. I brought an umbrella—so the lemonade didn't get ruined when it rained." "It helped me understand some of the things companies do. It's more complicated than I thought." "Trying this program helped me know what I should talk about with my mom. I was better prepared. She told me that she was proud of her little businesswoman." "It was fun—it helped me learn things, rather than just telling me."

Computer programs can be used to combine classroom work with community service/learning, and parents and educators should look for software that permits this kind of combination. Simulations such as Sell Lemonade are exactly what is needed to enhance these powerful learning experiences.

COMPUTER-LANGUAGE PROGRAMS

Some youngsters will spend much of their computer time learning to program. There are a variety of languages available—BASIC, LOGO, Pascal, FORTH, FORTRAN—each with its own proponents. Computers are changing so rapidly that it's almost impossible to tell which is the "best" language to learn. Most computers come with the BASIC language built in. They are ready to be programmed by people who know how to use it.

A decade ago a user needed to be able to program in order to get much use from a computer. Today it's completely unnecessary to know programming to get considerable use and enjoyment from computers. Before buying a particular language for your home computer, check with the school to see what they are using and talk with your child's teacher. Don't push your child to learn programming. Many people—adults and children who might otherwise have enjoyed using computers—have been discouraged by their failure to grasp programming. It's a valuable but certainly not mandatory skill.

Some educators insist that young people ought to learn LOGO. They see it not just as a computer language, but as an opportunity to improve the way young people learn, how they view themselves, and the way adults and students interact in schools. In the schools that make sophisticated use of LOGO, each of these things is happening. The students view computers as a tool to help complete complicated projects. Young people who enjoy LOGO are developing a better self concept. Students and teachers are helping each other, and students are serving as resources for each other. In one urban junior high school, a student who has mastered LOGO explained, "This makes me think I can learn other important things. I used to think that I was stupid. But when people ask me for help, I know that I'm not dumb—I'm good at some things—other people are good at different things."

Does this mean everyone should learn LOGO? Not necessarily. Learning to write a program using LOGO is something like learning to speak Spanish, repair an engine, write a poem, draw a picture, or build a wooden cabinet. Some people do each of these things much better than most of us. Others don't have as much natural ability but become intrigued, excited, and ultimately enthralled by the activity. Folks who have either natural ability or a strong interest find success in these endeavors. As Linda Mohn, an outstanding St. Paul kindergarten teacher explained, "LOGO turns on the lights for some kids. And other kids are not particularly interested. We need to challenge and stimulate everyone."

Unfortunately, the value of LOGO may be overstated. One national reviewer, for instance, insisted, "LOGO, as a language, is a useful tool that should be employed by any teacher interested in stimulating the creative processes in a student" (Stanton et al, p. 226). Now really! Should teachers of music, painting, sculpture, woodshop, home economics, or French, each of whom is trying to stimulate creativity, use LOGO? Not necessarily. Comments like this inevitably irritate and frustrate people who are working hard (and effectively) in other ways to encourage creativity.

More than a few parents with computers have asked, "Should I worry if my child doesn't seem very interested in LOGO?" The answer is no. Demanding that their children master LOGO, BASIC, or any other language is as productive as demanding that they spend hours practicing the piano, throwing a football, or perfecting needlepoint. A few children will appreciate their parents' demands. Most children will end up hating the activity they were forced to continue after their own interest ended.

TELECOMMUNICATION

Parents may wish to purchase software that permits their computer to communicate with various databases, which are something like electronic libraries. Organizations like the Source gather information on a vast array of subjects. Computer users may examine information in these databases by paying a certain hourly fee. Many areas also have what are called "electronic bulletin boards." Sometimes the people who establish these bulletin boards charge people to read them; sometimes reading them is free. Computer users connect to these by using local telephone lines. Getting and sending information over phone lines requires the purchase of a modem, a small machine that enables one computer to communicate with other computers via telephones. This is an advanced use of computers worth discussing with a salesperson and your children. Because there are often fees for using databases, purchasing this type of software opens up an additional, continuing expense. Be prepared!

Teenagers who've mastered word processing might be encouraged to learn database management and electronic forecasting. These are sophisticated skills that are vital in many careers. However, the technology is changing rapidly (becoming much easier to learn), so hold off buying this kind of software unless your youngsters have already developed many other computer-related skills.

LEARNING ABOUT
HIGH-QUALITY SOFTWARE

Deciding which basic categories of software to buy is only part of the process that parents and schools must go through. Since there are thousands of programs to choose from, most of us are going to need some guidance in finding the best programs available. Millions of dollars are spent on advertising, but consumers need more accurate, unbiased information than is found in ads. There are several sources of such information.

User groups. User groups can be an effective resource. In addition to helping you learn much more about your computer, the groups can tell you about low-cost software often available only through them. User groups have also performed critical consumer protection functions. Several groups arranged for service programs after the company producing their computer discontinued a model or went out of business. Some groups have arranged discounts and obtained other benefits for their members. How does one find out about nearby user groups? It's worth asking people in charge of computing in your local school district. Sometimes these educators have helped start user groups, or know how to contact them. Computer stores in many large cities can provide referrals. Writing directly to the company that manufactured your machine will help. The companies know about some of the largest local and national user groups. In some cities publications (such as *Computer User* in Minneapolis-St. Paul) provide information about user groups, and user groups frequently have displays at computing conferences in some of the largest cities.

Magazines. Magazines geared to the computer market usually publish reviews of software in each issue, and some of them annually print lists of the best educational software available. (The Resources section at the end of this book includes the names and addresses of a number of magazines, plus an assessment of each.) In the last few years, magazines have emerged that confine their reviews to particular machines. These publications provide the most information about what's available for that machine, but many of them are having a difficult time surviving.

Books. Books devoted entirely to software reviews are published, but they are probably not a good investment for most families because the information they contain is often outdated by the time they reach the public. New programs come out constantly, and the prices fall. No books can be rushed into print fast enough to keep up with all these changes, so consumers should consider carefully before purchasing any books consisting exclusively of software reviews.

Libraries. Libraries can be a wellspring of software information. It's unlikely that most schools or families will subscribe to all the publications that focus on computer software. School and community libraries, however, are aware of the growing public interest in computers, and many of them are trying to increase their resources on the subject. Most libraries will subscribe to at least some of the magazines listed in the Resources section of this book. And, if you're lucky, your library will also subscribe to the Educational Products Information Exchange (EPIE) Courseware Profiles. This service is affiliated with Consumer's Union, and supported by grants from various foundations; many authorities think that EPIE has the highest quality evaluations available.

Endorsements. Endorsements are a controversial source of software information. For example, the National Education Association (NEA), the nation's largest teachers' organization, has started endorsing software products, but its evaluation procedures have been criticized. To be reviewed by the NEA, software producers must pay the organization a fee. Some producers say they cannot afford the NEA charges and think them inappropriate. (Think of what would happen in this country if newspapers, magazines, and organizations began charging publishers who wanted books reviewed. Books would be reviewed only if the publisher could afford to pay.) Other questions have been raised regarding conflict of interest and impartiality of judgment.

Officials of the NEA defend the practice of charging software producers for reviews. "We pay teachers to do evaluations. Our assessments are quite unlike magazine software reviews. They are a good deal more complex and structured. We make sure they are tried in schools as part of the assessment process," explained Lawrence Fedewa, head of the NEA Educational Computer Service. He thinks it is appropriate to charge companies for this service. Nancy Kochuk, general spokesperson for NEA, feels that "reviewing is a way to get more publicity for software. It is a kind of advertising. The whole point of the review is to encourage software producers to meet standards. We serve as a kind of final quality control check for companies." They discounted the ill effects of the policy on software producers, pointing out, in Kochuk's words, that "participation is voluntary. Software producers can choose not to send their material to us, and to just use traditional reviewers." Both officials stressed that profits from the sale of NEA-approved software do not come to NEA. Any profits now go to the software producers and to Cordatum, the company that distributes software. Asked whether it's a conflict of interest for teachers who are members of NEA to be deciding between NEA-endorsed and other software, Fedewa replied "it's a free country."

Kochuk noted that several companies had improved their software as a result of NEA assessments. One company prepared material for third graders, but had used eighth-grade vocabulary. After getting NEA's written evaluation, the company revised its product. Another company called a press conference to praise the NEA service, explaining that it viewed the NEA procedure as a "final quality control check."

But while NEA officials appear to have the best of intentions, their procedures are ill-advised. Whether NEA is providing a consulting or a reviewing service seems a matter of some confusion. It's one thing if NEA wants to charge producers so that teachers can be paid to test software and make recommendations that the companies can use to revise and improve their software. Businesses and school districts frequently hire consultants to make recommendations for improvement. But it's probably inappropriate to ask the consultant (who has made recommendations on how to improve your product or service) to then tell the public why it should buy your product. The public needs reviewers who are, to the maximum extent possible, unbiased and objective.

DECIDING WHAT'S BEST
FOR YOUR CHILDREN OR STUDENTS

One of the most clear, comprehensive, and valuable set of criteria for rating software ratings has been developed by the authors of the *Book of Apple Software 1984*. (These authors also write similar books on IBM and Atari software.) Though individuals might not find the books a good investment, they are excellent additions to public libraries, at least until software evaluations are available electronically. The book's more than five hundred pages describe software in many categories, and one-hundred-and-eighty pages are devoted to teaching reading, math, science, typing, programming, and how computers function. The authors rate software on the following criteria:

Value for money. Is the software a good value compared to comparable programs?

Vendor support. Is the producer reliable in terms of answering questions about the software and replacing defective products?

Documentation. Does the material accompanying the disk do a clear and comprehensive job of explaining how to operate the system?

Error handling. Are there problems while the program is being operated? If so, does the program explain clearly what the problem is?

Reliability. Does the program do what it says it will do?

Visual appeal. Are the program's graphics interesting and well done?

Educational value. Does the program do an effective job of what it is supposed to teach?

Ease of use. Can the new user operate the program with a minimum of difficulty, or does it take a long time to learn? Does the program have features that make it operate relatively slowly?

Overall rating. Taking into account all factors, how does the program rate?

Another set of criteria for evaluating software has been developed by the Minnesota Department of Education as part of its overall technology plan for state schools. The evaluation forms provided by the department are used to determine whether software is placed on the state's list of "high quality" software. Minnesota rates software in three broad areas—and technical characteristics—and asks a number of questions about each. (This is only a selection.)

Instructional
- Does the program have a well-defined purpose?
- Does it makes effective use of graphics, color, and sound to motivate the student and to highlight key points to be learned?
- Is the reading level appropriate for the intended audience?
- Can the "content of this package . . . be learned as well or better by using the microcomputer than by using another teaching strategy"?

Content
- Is the material accurate, current, appropriate?
- Is the material presented in a clear and concise manner?

Technical Characteristics
- Is the accompanying material that explains the program clear?
- Can the sound be turned off?
- Is the program text free from grammar, spelling, punctuation, and hyphenation errors?
- Can youngsters easily exit from the program, return to the beginning, or obtain instructions?
- Does the program use relevant computer capabilities? (Minnesota Department of Education, 1983).

Minnesota's complete three-page form is available from the state. Before spending twenty to four hundred dollars on a single package, parents and educators should strongly consider obtaining and using this evaluation form.

The California Department of Education has taken a different approach by asking computer-using teachers to develop a set of criteria that educators can use to evaluate software. The standards should be available in late 1985. San Mateo computer coordinator Leroy Finkel, who serves on the group developing the forms, says that California will use an unusual (and valuable) rating system. Educators will use three kinds of characteristics to evaluate software:

- Essential attributes (those that software must have to be considered for use in schools);
- Desirable attributes (those that make the software more attractive); and
- Indicators of excellence (those that make the software extremely effective and worthwhile).

California educators are also concerned about the implied or explicit lessons on race and sex that the software conveys. In the last decade educators have become more sensitive to this issue, and textbooks have made some progress in this area. Yet some of the software or accompanying material seems to ignore the need to represent all races and sexes.

An example is the widely publicized and promoted IBM program Writing to Read, developed for young children by John Henry Martin. Martin spent several years experimenting with a combination of computers, typewriters, and related activities, and the resulting program is effective. The Educational Testing Service found that kindergarten students who used it were doing a much better job of writing and reading (Howitt, p. 29).

But students using the program may also learn other, unintended lessons. If you examine the Writing to Read workbooks that accompany the software, you'll discover that all of the children pictured appear to be white. Also, the majority of the boys pictured in the booklets are active and happy—they're frequently shown jumping or running—while the few girls in the workbooks are depicted in passive roles.

A SUMMARY ON SELECTING SOFTWARE

Thousands of educational programs have been produced, and millions of words have been written about them. At the risk of adding a few more, here's a summary of my recommendations for buying software:

1. Consider the various functions that computers can perform. This includes programmming, drill-practice, word processing, spreadsheet analysis, simulations, tutorials, and building awareness of numbers, shapes, and letters.
2. Think about the young people who will be using the computer. What are their specific interests and needs? What are their skills? How patient are they?
3. Establish priorities. With limited funds available to purchase software, it is not possible to buy everything on the market. Reading, talking with other users, and doing some hard thinking will be required to make wise selections.
4. Determine criteria for selecting specific software in broad categories. For example, if people decide word processing is an important use of the computer, they must still determine which wordprocessing package to purchase from the many available.
5. Read reviews critically. Factors that are important to reviewers may not be important to you, and vice versa. Many parents and educators may be looking for programs that are both easy to understand and inexpensive. A piece of software that costs twenty-nine dollars may be much easier to understand and more likely to be used than one available for twenty-one dollars. Be sure that software evaluations cover topics important to you.
6. Try to examine a program before buying it. Some publishers and stores allow preview opportunities. Use these opportunities. After actually trying out the material, you may have a different reaction to it than the reviewers did.

7. Try to find software that ties into other learning activities. A simulation becomes much more valuable if it relates to a real experience a child is about to have. Word processing is exciting in and of itself. But if word-processing and graphics programs are used to produce a school newspaper, a commercial product, or a booklet describing a community's history, their value is enhanced many times.

Software can be educational, fun, and exciting. But it can't do everything. Computers and accompanying software are most useful as *part* of well-designed learning programs. Don't expect them to take the place of creative teaching and a warm, loving home environment. The best use of technology is to enhance our human creativity, not substitute for it.

12

CONCLUSION

The time has come to stop shopping for miracles and to start working with simple things.

—Harriet Bernstein,
Council for Basic Education

Nearly everyone agrees that computers have enormous potential. But the introduction of computers into homes, schools, and businesses is being accompanied by a public relations campaign that ignores the possible dangers of an overzealous reliance on computers. People are asking lots of questions about computers, but often they're not the questions that need to be asked.

In this book, I've tried to examine seven myths about computers:

1. Computers are neutral—they're just another tool.
2. There is such a thing as computer literacy, and every graduate of our schools needs to have it.
3. Using computers is the most effective way for most students to learn most subjects.
4. Computers will revolutionize our schools.
5. The lessons of the past about introducing new technology into schools are clear and obvious.
6. All responsible parents who can possibly afford it should buy computers for their children.
7. There is not much software that can be used effectively to increase learning.

Parents who care about schools, students, and teachers must study these myths carefully, make decisions about their validity, and then act upon those decisions. If concerned people don't do this—if *we* don't do this—our society will lose the opportunity to make the best possible use of a powerful, complicated technology. Accepting the myths wholesale will waste millions of dollars, limit young people's development, and frustrate many of our finest teachers.

The patterns of computer use in homes and schools are just starting to evolve. There is still time to change course, to head in different—and better—directions in the educational use of computers. One of the remarkable facts about our nation is that concerned citizens can affect the status quo. Thoughtful, creative people can disagree, confront, and triumph. We need to remember that when pondering the influence of computers in our lives.

The first central message of this book is that *widespread involvement is critical* as families and schools consider ways to use computers. Parents, community members, and teachers should not just rely on the opinions of experts. We all need to think about these issues and take action when it seems appropriate.

The second central message of this book is that *computers are not neutral*—they are not just powerful tools. Computers and other advanced technology will influence the way we think and organize our lives. This book was written by a person who did not have an "office." It has been a strange, unnerving experience "going to work" by kissing my wife and children, walking into a room next to our bedroom, closing the door, and turning on the computer.

In the future, many people may work in their homes, communicating by telephones and computers with coworkers and supervisors. Unions are concerned about what will happen to their members and to their organizations when that happens. National news reports that some corporations are already hiring people (generally women) to use computers in their homes to process forms, but some companies are not paying such workers as much per hour or providing comparable fringe benefits as they do for those who come to the factory or office to work. Are computers going to create a harsher economic class system?

Some wonder if we will need school buildings in the future. Will it be feasible to communicate with many young children electronically? Certainly *Sesame Street* shows how it is possible to use television to teach important concepts. Computers could be combined with *Sesame Street* and its descendants to determine how many children are mastering the concepts presented. Those who do will be permitted to move ahead. Those who don't could receive additional lessons.

The third central message of this book is that *to make the most effective use of computers to help children learn, our educational programs must make major changes in structure.* In a few communities, schools are recognizing that in order to make the most sophisticated use of computers, they must employ people who do not have traditional teaching certificates. School districts must also create new kinds of career opportunities if they wish to retain the finest instructors. Some states are recognizing that much of the best information about how to use computers is being generated by classroom instructors. Educators and policymakers must break out of the rut that says that if we want teachers to learn something, we must require them to take a university course on the subject.

The kinds of questions we ask about computers and learning will influence the kind of answers we obtain. For some time people have been asking, "What can computers do for me? How can computers help teach the content I've been covering with textbooks and filmstrips?" It's time now to ask other questions.

The first new question ought to be, *"How can computers help young people work with and serve others?"* In the process of providing assistance to others, young people will learn basic and applied skills. Equally important, they will gain greater confidence in themselves and their abilities to improve the world.

- That's what happened in Ortonville, Minnesota, where teenagers used computers to make their family farms operate more efficiently.
- That's what happened in Folsom, Pennsylvania, where teenagers used computers to help families decide how to make their homes more energy-efficient.
- That's what happened in Tucson, Arizona, where students with learning disabilities learned to create adventure games on computers. Other students then began to view these kids in different ways, and they began to see themselves as more worthwhile people.

The second new question we ought to ask is, *"How can computers be used to encourage individual creativity?"*

- That's what's happened in computer labs where students learn to improve their writing via word processing. All over the country teachers report that students show more enthusiasm and creativity in their writing because word processing makes writing more enjoyable.
- That's what happened in Hartford, Connecticut, where an extraordinary teacher worked with students to develop learning games. His students expanded and developed their creativity as they thought about ways to teach others about community resources.

The third question ought to be, *"How should schools change staffing patterns to attract and keep outstanding people working with students?"*

- That's what happened in Houston, where outstanding teachers were paid more money and given additional responsibilities if they remained in the classroom and agreed to work in schools with students from low-income families.
- That's what happened in New York, where the district identified outstanding teachers, hired them to teach

other faculty after school, and developed cooperative relationships with universities. These teachers retain their contact with youngsters in classrooms, while also functioning as adjunct university professors.

The fourth new question ought to be, *"What computer applications are being developed for home and business use that can be used to help youngsters gain self-confidence and competence?"*

- That's the question Delores and Budd Hagen asked. It led them to help thousands of handicapped and disabled people.
- That's the question Minnesota Department of Education official Gil Valdez asked. He's now encouraging schools to help students learn to gather information electronically, conduct research in libraries far from their homes, and apply word-processing techniques to improve writing.

A fifth new question should be, *"How can we ensure access to sophisticated uses of computers for students from low-income families?"*

- That's the question Houston asked. It has taken a series of steps to work with low-income parents and their children that should be studied and adapted throughout the nation. Houston has made dramatic changes in its relationship to parents, and in the way learning is organized. It's recognized that there is no one best educational program for all students.
- That's the question the Minneapolis Public Library asked. It has started a software checkout system. Patrons are able to borrow computer software just as they borrow books.

A sixth question ought to be, *"How can we make more efficient use of existing resources?"*

- That's the question Robbinsdale, Minnesota, educators asked when the district decided to locate its Technology Learning Campus in a building that also housed other programs serving the community.
- That's the question Henderson, Minnesota, officials asked when they decided to provide vacant space in

the high school in return for training and access to Budd and Delores Hagen's computer lab.

A 1982 federal study reports what many of us believe, "The nation's educational needs are not now being met." But then, in a classic example of computer hype, the document asserts that the "new information technologies offer a promising mechanism, and in some cases *the only mechanism*, for responding to these educational needs" (Office of Technology Assessment, p. 182 —emphasis added).

We should never view machines as the only answer to our problems. Computers should spur us to ask new questions, to seek new answers. Those answers will come not from machines, but from people—the people who are in charge of the machines, who respect their capabilities, and who value most highly human abilities.

If we place machines at the center, we will have missed their potential. If we decide that the primary use of educational computers is to drill youngsters, we will have misused their capabilities. If we ignore issues of equity, we'll move farther from their capacity to move the whole society ahead. The five years from 1985 to 1990 will produce patterns. Parents and educators in the twenty-first century may well look back on that period as a key. New patterns are possible. New ways are being considered.

Computers have created new challenges, new opportunities—but no guarantees. It's up to people who care about kids to accept the responsibility. As a statesman once observed, "We may not be able to change the past, but we can help to shape the future."

A SUMMARY OF SUGGESTIONS
Having computers available is no guarantee that they will be used wisely. People sometimes mistakenly assume that all progress requires money. Some of the actions recommended below require no outlay of

money; some require a bit of spending; and some require substantial investments (or reallocation of existing resources). All are steps worth considering:

1. Information about Computers and Software

- Ignore products whose commercials encouraging the purchase of computers or software are based on fear and insecurity. Notify companies of your feelings about their advertisements.
- Encourage libraries to obtain software reviews. These should be available in both print and electronic form in order to include the most recent releases. Federal and foundation support should encourage development and implementation of such programs, ensuring that they are available in low-income neighborhoods.
- Insist that any organization publishing reviews disclose financial dealings between reviewers and the products being reviewed.
- Encourage and assist libraries, particularly in low-income neighborhoods, to purchase computers and software that can be made available to library patrons, along with training and discussion of the impact of computers and other advanced technology.

2. Educational Practices

- Insist that school policies be modified to permit employment of people who are not certified teachers but who have expertise with computing.
- Encourage the use of shared facilities so that educational funds can be used most efficiently, and advanced technology can be made available to the widest possible population.
- Encourage the development of alternatives and options.
- Provide summer programs using various applications of computers for as many young people as are interested.
- Insist that all students have opportunities to use computers in school computer labs.
- Help teachers who are responsible for writing instruction learn to use word processing.
- Help elementary students learn to type.

- Encourage the use of computers to help solve real-world problems.
- Encourage educational use of applications developed to solve business or social problems (e.g., word processing, database management, and other applications).
- Provide opportunities for teachers to experiment with new applications of computers.
- Expand career options for teachers so that they can work part-time with students and part time in other fields, such as corporate computer use, training, research, etc.
- Examine software rigorously.
- Avoid the computer literacy approach. Instead, give priority to using computers throughout the curriculum in sophisticated ways, such as word processing, simulation, computer-assisted design, spreadsheet analysis, etc.
- Require students to demonstrate before graduation an understanding of the ways in which technology influences how people think, communicate, and act.
- Set up computer labs in all elementary schools. At least fifty percent of the time available on computers should be devoted to word processing. Young people should have opportunities to use computers in various ways in the primary grades.
- Attempt to have computer supervision provided by staff of both sexes and as many races as possible. Students must see from their first encounters with computers that the machines are not the exclusive province of white males.

3. Research Emphasis
- The greatest attention and support should be given to programs that employ both university scholars and classroom practitioners.
- One high priority for software development should be to create material that permits computers to be used to develop "higher order thinking skills": analysis of problems, gathering information about problems, developing tentative conclusions about ways to solve problems, trying out possible conclusions, evaluating results, and using this information.

- Another priority should be investigating the ways that the increased reliance on computers could affect human development and communication.
- A third priority ought to be identifying the special strengths and needs of rural students.

4. Use of Computers in the Home

- Families should not rush to purchase computers out of a sense of guilt or insecurity.
- Families should have a clear understanding of the ways a computer will be used in their home before considering buying one.
- Parents who are going to purchase computers should be willing to spend significant time learning about them.
- Families should study ways in which computers can foster group activities, rather than increase isolation within the family. Cooperative activities could include attending computer shows, learning various applications, taking courses, playing games, deciding which software to purchase, etc.

5. Evaluation of Computers' Impact

- Any evaluation of student knowledge about computers should include actual demonstration of skills. Paper-pencil knowledge is not enough. Limiting assessment to these kinds of tests will encourage a much more limited development of skill.
- In assessing the impact of computers, evaluators should look for several factors in addition to higher scores on standardized tests. These factors should include (1) increased student enthusiasm for learning, (2) improved student attitudes toward school, (3) better relationships between students and faculty, (4) better use of faculty skills, and (5) strong student skills in analyzing, researching, creating, and problem-solving.

RESOURCES

Anderson, Ronald. "Computer Equity." *Computer User,* November 1984, 26.

_____. "National Computer Literacy, 1980." In *Computer Literacy: Issues and Directions for 1985,* edited by Robert Seidel, Ronald Anderson, and Beverly Hunter. New York: Academic Press, 1982.

_____. "Statement Before the Subcommittee on Investigations and Oversight of the House Science and Technology Committee," September 29, 1983 (mimeographed).

Barbour, Andrew, and editors of *Electronic Learning.* "Computing in America's Classrooms 1984." *Electronic Learning,* October 1984, 39-44.

Barstow, Daniel. "Urban Adventure." *Popular Computing,* August 1983, 98-102.

Bartimo, Jim. "The Art of Buying a Computer." *Infoworld,* October 22, 1984, 27-31.

Becker, Henry Jay. "How Schools Use Micro-Computers." *Classroom Computer Learning,* September 1983, 41-44.

_____. "School Use of Micro-Computers." Quoted in "Location of Micros Seen to Affect Use, Effectiveness." *Electronic Learning,* September 1984, 18.

Bergen, Steve, and Schairman, Lynne. "Who's Pushing the Buttons." *Classroom Computer News,* November-December 1984, 52-55.

Bernstein, Harriet T. "The Information Society: Byting the Hand That Feeds You." *Phi Delta Kappan,* October 1983, 108-109.

Bonner, Paul. "Computers in Education, Promise and Reality." *Personal Computing,* September 1984, 64.

_____. "Coping with the Silicon Syndrome." *Personal Computing,* May 1984, 82.

Bowe, Frank. "Micros and Special Education." *Popular Computing,* mid-October 1984, 121-128.

Boyer, Ernest. "Education's New Challenge." *Personal Computing,* September 1984, 81-85.

—————. *High School: A Report on Secondary Education in America.* New York: Harper & Row, 1983.

Brady, Holly. "Don't Think Computers, Think Kids." *Classroom Computer News,* September 1983, 6.

Brumbaugh, Ken, and Rawitsch, Don. *Establishing Instructional Computing: The First Steps.* St. Paul: Minnesota Educational Computing Consortium, 1982.

Camp, John. "Computers Help Handicapped See the Light." *St. Paul Sunday Pioneer Press,* December 16, 1984, 11-12H.

Chin, Kathy. "IBM Funds Teacher Training." *Infoworld,* October 22, 1984, 15.

Chion-Kenney, Linda. "Computer, School, Family in Houston: A 'Total Commitment'" *Education Week,* November 7, 1984, 1, 11.

Coburn, Peter; Kelman, Peter; Roberts, Nancy; Snyder, Thomas F. F.; Watt, Daniel; and Weiner, Cheryl. *Practical Guide to Computers in Education.* Reading, Mass.: Prentice-Hall, 1982.

Collins, Glenn. "Home Computers Found to Reinforce Family Patterns." *Minneapolis Star and Tribune,* October 14, 1984, 1F.

Congressional Research Service. *Information Technology in Education: Perspectives and Potentials.* Washington, D.C.: U.S. Government Printing Office, 1981.

Cooper, William John. *Annual Report of the Commissioner of Education for the Fiscal Year Ended June 30, 1983.* Washington, D.C.: U.S. Government Printing Office, 1932, 29.

Covvey, H. Dominic, and McAlister, Neil Harding. *Computer Choices.* Reading, Mass.: Addison-Wesley, 1982.

Cutler, Ivan. "Designing the Office around the Computer." *Personal Computing,* November 1984, 84-86.

Dearman, Nancy B., and Plisko, Valena White, eds. *The Condition of Education.* 1982 ed. Washington, D.C.: National Center for Education Statistics, 1982.

Deringer, Dorothy K., and Molnar, Andrew. "Key Components for a National Computer Literacy Program." In *Computer Literacy,* edited by Robert Seidel, Ronald

Anderson, and Beverly Hunter. New York: Academic Press, 1982.

Dunn, Rita, and Dunn, Kenneth. "Learning Styles/Teaching Styles: Should They . . . Can They Be Matched?" *Educational Leadership*, January 1979.

Dyrli, Odvard Egil. "Review Slingers for Hire." *Classroom Computer Learning*, October 1984.

Fawcette, James. "All You Need to Learn about Programming." *Personal Computing*, December 1984, 183-186.

Fine, Benjamin. *Teaching Machines*. New York: Sterling Publishing Co., 1962.

Finkel, Leroy. Speech at Minnesota Educational Computing Corporation conference, November 1984.

Fisher, Glenn. "Where CAI Is Effective." *Electronic Learning*, November-December 1983, 82-84.

Fiske, Edward. "Computers, in Most Schools, Have Brought No Revolution." *New York Times*, December 9, 1984, 1.

Forman, Denyse. "Search of the Literature." *The Computing Teacher*, January 1982, 37-51.

Friedland, Edward. "Letter to the Editor." *Classroom Computer News*, September 1983, 8.

Furst, Miriam. "Enabling Learning Disabled Children to Become Facilitators of Learning." *Closing the Gap*, October-November 1984, 1.

Futrell, Mary Hatwood. "Quality Education Demands Quality Software." *Education Week*, December 12, 1984, 10.

Galanter, Eugene. *Kids and Computers*. New York: Perigee Books, 1983.

Gallup, George H. "16th Annual Gallup Poll of the Public's Attitudes toward the Public Schools." *Phi Delta Kappan*, September 1984, 31.

Gartner, Alan; Kohler, Mary Conway; and Riessman, David. *Children Teach Children*. New York: Harper & Row, 1971.

Goodlad, John. "What Some Schools and Classrooms Teach." *Educational Leadership*, April 1983, 8-19.

Grady, David. "Lack of Respect Is No Joke." *Computer Update*, March-April 1983, 65-67.

Greenfield, Patricia Marks. *Mind and Media: The Effects of Television, Video Games and Computers*. Cambridge: Harvard Univ. Press, 1984.

Guilbeau, John J. "Micros for the Special Ed Administrator." *Electronic Learning*, February 1984, 43.

Hagen, Delores. *Microcomputer Resource Book for Special Education*. Reston, Va.: Reston Publishing Co., 1984.

Hartnell, Tim. "The Great Personal Computer Con." *Creative Computing*, November 1984, 197-200.

Hassett, James. "Computers in Classrooms." *Psychology Today*, September 1984, 22-28.

Hoffman, Irwin. "When Computer Literacy Metamorphosis Is Complete. . . . " *Electronic Education*, November-December 1984, 18.

Hollands, Jean. *The Silicon Syndrome: A Survival Handbook for Couples*. Palo Alto: Coastlight Press, 1984.

Howe, Harold II. "Computers, The New Kick in Schools." *College Board Review*, Summer 1983, 24-32.

Howitt, Doran. "Database Confusion Reigns." *Infoworld*, July 16, 1984, 37.

_____. "Experimental Software Boosted." *Infoworld*, October 29, 1984, 29.

Hunter, Beverly. *Personal Computers and Social Education*. Cupertino, Calif.: Apple Computer Co., 1984.

_____. "Problem Solving with Data Bases." *The Computing Teacher*, May 1985, 20-27.

Kidder, Tracy. *The Soul of a New Machine*. New York: Avon Books, 1981.

Komonski, P. Kenneth. "Educational Computing: The Burden of Insuring Quality." *Phi Delta Kappan*, December 1984, 244-250.

Kulik, James. "Synthesis of Research on Computer-Based Instruction." *Educational Leadership*, September 1983, 19-21.

Lengel, James G. *Computer Considerations for Vermont Schools*. Montpelier, Vt.: Vermont Department of Education, 1983.

Levin, Henry; Glass, Gene; and Meister, Gail. *Cost Effectiveness of Four Educational Interventions*. Stanford: Institute for Research on Educational Finance and Governance, May 1984, Report 84-A11.

Loebl, Dina, and Kantrov, Ilene. "Micros in the Special Ed Classroom." *Electronic Learning*, February 1984, 38-39.

Luerhrmann, Arthur. "Word Processing for Girls, Programming for Boys, Right?" Speech at Minnesota Educational Computing Corporation conference, Minneapolis, November 1984.

Luerhrmann, Arthur, and Peckham, Herbert. *Computer Literacy, A Hands-On Approach.* New York: McGraw-Hill, 1983.

Lundstrom, Peter. *A Personal Guide to Personal Computers.* Cupertino, Calif.: Apple Computer Co., 1982.

Mace, Scott. "'Certification' Questioned." *Infoworld,* October 29, 1984, 46-47.

Mako, Ed. Unpublished specialist degree paper, St. Thomas University, 1985.

Minnesota Educational Computing Corporation. *Highlight Report: A Study of Computer Use and Literacy in Science Education.* Minneapolis: MECC, 1980.

Moursund, Dave. "NEA and Educational Software." *The Computing Teacher,* October 1984, 4-5.

National Commission on Excellence in Education. *A Nation at Risk.* Washington, D.C.: U.S. Government Printing Office, 1983.

National Education Association Educational Computer Service. *Guide to the Software Assessment Procedure Reviewer Document #1: Courseware.* Washington, D.C.: National Education Association Educational Computer Service, 1983.

_____. *The Yellow Book of Computer Products for Education.* (Summer Supplement, 1984). Washington, D.C.: NEA Educational Computer Service, 1984.

National School Boards Association. *School/Home Computer Survey.* Alexandria, Va.: NSBA, 1984.

New York City Public Schools. *Computer Literacy: Elementary Grades.* New York: Board of Education of the City of New York, 1983.

_____. *Computer Literacy: Intermediate and Secondary Grades.* New York: Board of Education of the City of New York, 1983.

Noble, Douglas. "Jumping off the Computer Bandwagon." *Education Week,* October 3, 1984, 21-24.

O'Brien, Peggy. "Using Microcomputers in the Writing Class." *The Computing Teacher,* May 1984, 20-21.

Office of Technology Assessment. *Informational Technology and Its Impact on American Education.* Washington, D.C.: U.S. Government Printing Office, 1982.

Ohanian, Susan. "How Today's Reading Software Can Zap Kid's Desire to Read." *Classroom Computer Learning,* November-December 1984, 28-31.

Orlansky, Jesse. "Effectiveness of CAI, A Different Finding." *Electronic Learning,* September 1983, 58-60.

Palmer, Adelaide; Dowd, Thomas; and James, Katherine. "Changing Teacher and Student Attitudes Through Word Processing." *The Computing Teacher,* May 1984, 45-47.

Papert, Seymour. *Mindstorms.* New York: Basic Books, 1980.

_____. "Misconceptions about LOGO." *Creative Computing,* November 1984, 229-230.

Pask, Gordon, with Curran, Susan. *Micro Man: Computers and the Evolution of Consciousness.* New York: Macmillan, 1982.

Phillipo, John. "Industry and the Public Schools: A Partnership That Can Work." *American Education,* November 1983, 28-29.

Pogrow, Stanley. "Computers and Education: State Policy Issues." July 20, 1983 (mimeographed).

Quality Education Data. *Micro-Computer Usage in Schools.* Denver: Quality Education Data, 1984.

Roblyer, M. D. "Measuring the Impact of Computers in Instruction: A Review of Research and Research Needs." Speech at MECC '84, Minneapolis, November 29, 1984.

Rutherford, F. James. "Testimony of H.R. 3750 and H.R. 4628 before the Subcommittee on Science, Research, and Technology." June 5, 1984 (mimeographed).

Seidel, Robert; Anderson, Ronald; Hunter, Beverly. *Computer Literacy.* New York: Academic Press, 1982.

Shavelson, Richard; Winkler, John; Stasz, Cathleen; Feibel, Werner; Robyn, Abby; and Shaha, Steven. *Teaching Mathematics and Science: Patterns of Microcomputer Use.* Santa Monica: Rand Corporation, 1984.

Sherman, Kenneth B. "Computer Literacy and Test Patterns." *Wall Street Journal,* September 11, 1984, 36.

Simon, Herbert. "Computers in Education: Realizing the Potential." *American Education,* December 1983, 17-23.

Sloan, Douglas. "On Raising Critical Questions about the Computer in Education." *Teachers College Record* 85, no. 4 (Summer 1984), 539-47.

Smith, Penny. "Preschoolers Learn at Home." *Creative Computing*, October 1984, 52-61.

Sproull, Lee; Kiesler, Sara; Zubrow, David. *Encountering an Alien Culture*. Pittsburgh: Carnegie-Mellon University, 1984 (mimeographed).

Stanton, Jeffrey; Wells, Robert; Rochowansky, Sandra; and Mellin, Michael, eds. *The Book of Apple Software 1984*. Los Angeles: The Book Company, 1984.

Sturdivant, Patricia. "Access to Technology: The Equity Paradox." *The Computing Teacher*, April 1984, 65-67.

TALMIS. "U.S. Consumer Demand for Home Computers: How Many Will Buy." Chicago: TALMIS, 1984.

Taylor, Robert, ed. *The Computer in the School: Tutor, Took, Tutee*. New York: Teachers College Press, 1980.

Tucker, Marc. *Computers in the Schools: The Federal Role*. Washington, D.C.: Project on Information Technology and Education, 1983 (mimeographed).

Turkle, Sherry. *The Second Self: Computers and the Human Spirit*. New York: Simon and Schuster, 1984.

Turner, Rebecca. "Computer Certification for Teachers: Three States Lead the Way." *Learning*, March 1984, 55.

Watt, Daniel. "Update on LOGO." In *Popular Computing Guide to Computers in Education*, mid-October 1984, 66-67.

_____. "Education for Citizenship in a Computer-Based Society." In *Computer Literacy: Issues and Directions for 1985*, edited by Seidel, Robert; Anderson, Ronald; and Hunter, Beverly. New York: Academic Press, 1982.

Watt, Peggy. "Computers Give Independence to the Disabled." *Infoworld*, March 19, 1984, 30-31.

Weizenbaum, Joseph. "A Rebel in the Computer Revolution." *Science Digest*, August 1983, 94-97.

White, George T, Jr. "Micros for the Special Ed Administrator." *Electronic Learning*, February 1984, 40-41.

Willett, Edward; Swanson, Austin; and Nelson, Eugene. *Modernizing the Red Schoolhouse: The Economics of Improved Education*. Englewood Cliffs, N.J.: Educational Technology Publications, 1979.

Williams, Frederick, and Williams, Victoria. *Growing up with Computers: A Parents' Survival Guide*. New York: Quill, 1983.

Zarley, Craig. "The Pleasures and Perils of Computing at Home." *Personal Computing*, May 1984, 76-83.

——————. "Computer Total Doubles in Largest School Districts." *Teaching and Computers,* January 1985, 6.

COMPUTER SOFTWARE
(Prices are not given because they change frequently.)
Addison-Wesley, Computer Math Activities.
Apple Computer Co., Apple-Writer.
Broderbund Software, Print Shop.
International Business Machines, Writing to Read.
Minnesota Educational Computing Corp., Marketplace.
——————, Path Tactics.
——————, The Friendly Computer.
Scarborough Software, Inc., MasterType.
Scholastic, Inc., Bank Street Writer.
——————, Story Maker: A Fact and Fiction Tool Kit.
Simon and Schuster, Typing Tutor III.
Software Publishing Corp., PFS:File, PFS:Report, PFS:Graph.
South-Western Publishing Co., MicroType, the Wonderful World of Paws.
Spinnaker Software Corp., Kidwriter.
Springboard Software, Inc., Early Games for Young Children.
——————, Mask Parade.
——————, The Newsroom.
Sunburst, The Factory.
——————, Getting Ready to Read and Add.
——————, Magic Slate.

INTERVIEWS
With students, educators, corporate officials, and parents in Alaska, Bermuda, California, Connecticut, Illinois, Indiana, Iowa, Manitoba, Massachusetts, Minnesota, Nebraska, New York, Texas, Vermont, Wisconsin, and Washington, D.C. People change positions, and projects go in new directions (or sometimes end). As of mid-1985, additional information about projects described is available by contacting:
Scott Williams, McKinley Alternative School, P.O. Box 1250, Fairbanks, Ala. 99701.
Dan Barstow, c/o Gifted/Talented Office, Webster School, 5 Cone St., Hartford, Conn. 06105. (203) 722-8931.

Mike Fields, c/o Project C.O.F.F.E.E., Oxford HS Annex, Main St., Oxford, Mass. 01540. (617) 987-2591.

Leroy Finkel, San Mateo COE, 333 Main St., Redwood City, Calif. 94063. (415) 363-5484.

Gary Honken, Project BEACON, 6th and Galbraith, Blue Earth, Minn. 56013. (507) 526-3215.

Ed Mako, c/o Lakeville Senior High School, 19544 Kenwood Trail, Lakeville, Minn. 55044. (612) 469-4461.

Phillip Nelson, University of Northern Iowa, Cedar Falls, Ia. 50613. (319) 268-0694.

Coordinator, Summatech, c/o North Community High School, 1500 James Avenue N., Minneapolis, Minn. 55411. (612) 627-2778, ext. 213.

Burton Nypen, c/o Ortonville Public Schools, 200 N. Sixth, Ortonville, Minn. 56278.

Barbara Nemer, Technology Learning Campus, 4139 Regent Avenue N., Robbinsdale, Minn. 55422. (612) 535-1790.

Nick Ignatuk, Project Detect, Ridley School District, Administration Building, 1001 Morton Ave., Folsom, Pa. 19033.

Mike Ryan, Director, Computer and Information Science Unit, New York City Public Schools, Room 409, 131 Livingston St., Brooklyn, N.Y. 11201.

Dr. Patricia Sturdivant, Houston Independent School District, Dept. of Technology, 5300 San Felipe, Houston, Tex. 77056.

STRONGLY RECOMMENDED RESOURCES

The following resources do not include magazines oriented to a particular machine. There are magazines devoted exclusively to the major machines (Apple, Commodore, IBM, Atari, Radio Shack). These magazines start and stop frequently. Check with a nearby computer store or with the manufacturer to get accurate information.

The list also does not include all the magazines published about computing. But the list does include many of the highest quality and most widely read publications. Prices are not given for magazines because they frequently change.

1. **For general information about developments in computing,** with frequent articles about computing in homes and schools, and software reviews that include educational material:

Byte, 70 Main St., Peterborough, N.H. 03458. Monthly. A huge (often over 600 pages), sophisticated magazine. For those who are serious about the computer and its implications.

Creative Computing, 39 East Hanover Ave., Morris Plains, N.J. 07950. Monthly. One of the oldest and most respected general magazines. Includes articles that are somewhat more technical than the other magazines listed except *Byte.*

Infoworld, 1060 Marsh Road, Suite C-200, Menlo Park, Calif. 94025. Weekly. Includes news and gossip about the computer industry. Does not have a "gee whiz, aren't computers wonderful" attitude. Tries to identify exciting and disturbing developments.

Personal Computing, Hayden Publishing Company, Inc., 10 Mulholland Dr., Hasbrouck Heights, N.J. 07604. Monthly. Somewhat more oriented toward business than home or school computing, but has provocative articles and reviews.

2. **For educators:**

Classroom Computer Learning, 19 Davis Drive, Belmont, Calif. 94002. Nine issues per year. News, reviews, articles. Articles cover practical applications as well as controversies.

Electronic Learning, c/o Scholastic, Inc., 730 Broadway, New York, N.Y. 10003-9538. Eight issues per year. Devoted to educational uses of advanced technology, primarily computers. Articles, surveys, news, reviews.

Closing the Gap, P.O. Box 68, Henderson, Minn. 56044. (612) 248-3294. Six times per year. This magazine is published by parents of a handicapped child who have become recognized internationally as experts on use of computers with such young people and adults. It includes stories, reviews, and news. The style is informal and honest.

The Computing Teacher, c/o International Council for Computers in Education, University of Oregon, 1787 Agate

St., Eugene, Oreg. 97403-1923. Nine issues per year. Published by educators; articles, news surveys, reviews.

3. For families and libraries:

Closing the Gap, P.O. Box 68, Henderson, Minn. 56044. (612) 248-3294. Six times per year. This magazine is published by parents of a handicapped child who have become recognized internationally as experts on use of computers with such young people and adults. The magazine is informal, focused, clearly written, and honest. It includes articles by educators and parents.

Family Computing, c/o Scholastic, Inc., 730 Broadway, New York, N.Y. 10003-9538. Monthly. Another magazine, like *Electronic Learning*, published by Scholastic. Contains articles, news, reviews.

Popular Computing, 70 Main St., Peterborough, N.H. 03458. Monthly. Another magazine, like *Byte*, published by McGraw-Hill, Inc. Primarily oriented toward home use of computers, with some articles relating to schools and business.

4. For software reviews:

(These are not the only groups conducting software reviews for educational products. However, they are widely respected and worth investigating by libraries, school districts, educators, and parents who want thoughtful, objective reactions to software.)

Educational Products Information Exchange Institute, Box 839, Water Mill, N.Y. 11976.

MICROSIFT, c/o Northwest Regional Educational Laboratory, 300 S.W. 6th Ave., Portland, Oreg. 97204. (503) 248-6800.

Minnesota High Quality Courseware List, from Minnesota Curriculum Services Center, 3554 White Bear Ave., White Bear Lake, Minn. 55110. (612) 770-3943.

Minnesota Courseware Evaluation Form, from Harold McDermott, Minnesota Department of Education, 550 Cedar Ave., St. Paul, Minn. 55101. (612) 297-2534.

5. Also available:

National Educational Association Computer Service Guides to Software Assessment, c/o NEA Educational Computer Service, 4720 Montgomery Lane, Bethesda, Md.

20814-5383. (301) 951-9244. Note: The NEA Educational Computer Service Guide to the Software Assessment Procedure Reviewer Document #1 is one of four publications available showing how this organization reviews software. Also available are booklets on how to review applications software, how to review combination products, and how to review computer interactive video courseware.

INDEX

78030